British
Columbia's

Best
Camping
Adventures

*Northern, Central and
Southeastern BC*

Jayne Seagrave

HERITAGE HOUSE

Copyright © 1999 Jayne Seagrave

CANADIAN CATALOGUING IN PUBLICATION DATA

Seagrave, Jayne 1961-
British Columbia's Best Camping Adventures

ISBN 1-895811-76-7

1. Camp sites, facilities, etc.—British Columbia—Guidebooks
2. Outdoor recreation—British Columbia—Guidebooks
3. British Columbia—Guidebooks
I. Title.
GV191.46.B75S418 1999   917.11'044   C99-910161-7

First edition 1999

Heritage House wishes to acknowledge the Book Publishing Industry Development Program of Heritage Canada, and the British Columbia Arts Council.

Front Cover Photo: Helmcken Falls, Wells Gray Park
Back Cover Photos: Fintry, Yoho National, and Tyhee Lake

Photographs by Andrew Dewberry except for British Columbia Archives and Records Service (BCARS) I-05218, p. 83; BC Parks, pp. 91, 124, 142; A. McClellan, p. 30; and Heritage House, p. 80.
Design, layout, and maps by Darlene Nickull
Edited by Audrey McClellan

HERITAGE HOUSE PUBLISHING COMPANY LTD.
Unit #8 - 17921 55th Ave., Surrey, BC V3S 6C4

Printed in Canada

CONTENTS

FOREWORD

Each year I can't wait until spring, when the camping season arrives and I become reacquainted with the many beautiful provincial parks I adore. Since moving to B.C. in 1991 I have camped in over 100 provincial parks and visited all those with camping facilities. Over the last eight years my enthusiasm for the qualities they offer has not dissipated. On the contrary, I love the way the province I have chosen to call home is committed to extending and supporting the provincial park system.

In 1997 I wrote *Provincial and National Park Campgrounds in B.C.: A Complete Guide*. The book was an immediate success, confirming that my passion for camping in provincial parks was shared by millions of others. In 1998 *B.C.'s Best Camping Adventures: Southwestern B.C. and Vancouver Island* was published, providing detailed information on provincial park campgrounds easily accessible from the Lower Mainland. This third book completes the trilogy, giving data on the best campgrounds in northern, central, and southeastern B.C.

All three books have been written to encourage both novice and veteran campers to explore the wonderful facilities and breathtaking scenery the province offers.

Earlier this year my son Jack was born. I am looking forward to sharing with him the many fantastic provincial parks and encouraging him to share my passion by experiencing the best camping adventures in B.C.

INTRODUCTION

THE JOY OF CAMPING

What is it about a tent, a recreational vehicle (RV), or just sleeping outdoors that is so appealing to so many? I constructed my first tent when I was five—in the front room of my grandmother's house underneath a dining table draped with sheets and blankets. Here my brother, sister, and I hid from the adult world in our makeshift home. When I was slightly older I persuaded my parents to let us sleep outside in the back garden. I remember the planning and excitement of this first excursion as we decided what was needed for our night away: food, clothing, bedding, games, flashlights, etc. In retrospect, this planning was similar to that preceding my camping trips thirty years later.

I was raised in England, where the climate and population are not conducive to "getting away from it all" camping, so I did not camp with my family, but at the age of thirteen I spent my first week away from home in a tent on the Yorkshire Moors. I recall little about this excursion other than the rain that fell incessantly. It was at this point I realized that to enjoy camping I probably needed to move continents. At the age of eighteen I gained employment for three months at a summer camp for children in the Catskill Mountains of New York State. Here I learned about North American camping, about toasting marshmallows; making S'mores; cooking hot dogs, hamburgers, and sloppy Joes; lighting a campfire; and the pure magic of sleeping under the stars. Here it never rained. This was truly the land of camping opportunities.

Who Camps and Why?

Although the Aboriginal communities have been camping for centuries, what we regard as contemporary camping is a North American tradition of the twentieth century. The American Camping Association was formed in 1910 when camping had become an established pastime. Tom Huggler in *The Camper and Backpackers Bible* describes how the birth of the RV can be attributed to an event in 1916 when two well-known inventors, Henry Ford and Thomas Edison, decided to go out and camp in converted motor cars with two friends, naturalist John Burroughs and tire tycoon Henry Firestone. In his history of camping, Huggler goes on to quote from a book written in 1924 entitled *Camping Out: A Manual for Organised Camping*: "There is hardly an adult who does not long for the time when he can escape from the confining repressive environment of modern city civilisation to the freedom and simplicity of the open road and the camp, or to some place he can call his country." This sentiment is still true today for both men *and* women.

One of the things that amazes me about campers is that there is no common denominator. After years of camping I realize they come in all shapes and sizes, are from all walks of life, and fall into every age group. This is not a pursuit exclusively for the young or the rich or the slim or the beautiful. It does not depend on the best designer outfit or state-of-the-art equipment. You do not get "too old" for camping and you can do it on a small budget. I admit that at a certain age (and affluence level) many decide to trade in the tent for an RV, but the love of the outdoors and of food cooked on an open fire remains. No matter whether you lay your head on a Thermarest under canvas or on a cushioned bed in a $100,000 motor home, you are still a camper; you still go to sleep smelling

An idyllic and typical camping spot (Exchamsikr River).

of wood smoke and wake up to the early morning crackling of someone else's fire, content to enjoy a crisp, dewy environment on that first walk to the "thunderbox" (pit toilet).

Just as there is no archetypal camper, so there are a hundred and one reasons why people camp. One primary reason is of course economic. The six-person tent I purchased five years ago for $350 has saved me more than $6000 in motel bills and still has many more years of use left. Camping is affordable, and for families this is particularly appealing.

There are other advantages. It introduces people to the outdoors and the natural world and is therefore a fantastic educational process. Camping takes you away from the pressures of daily life. When you are camping, the biggest decision you have to make is what to have for dinner and the only clock-watching you need to do is to make sure to visit the thunderbox before it gets too dark and you cannot see where it is. Camping brings families and couples together in shared activities away from the flicker of a TV screen. Children take an active part in the experience. They go to collect wood and water, help erect the tents and washing lines, and then can be left to their own devices in a safe environment.

Camping is experiencing a boom as many seek ways to attain the simple things in life: clean air, the sound of waves lapping a shoreline, sunsets, and the smell of wood smoke.

In 1997, 2.7 million people visited provincial and national campgrounds in British Columbia, an increase of 12 percent over the previous five years. British Columbians comprised 65 percent of these campers (15 percent were Canadians from other provinces, 10 percent from the United States, and the rest from overseas). It is estimated that 60 million people on this continent, a quarter of the population, have camped at some time. The BC Parks system covers almost 9.5 million hectares, an area larger than New Brunswick, and in 1998 BC Parks announced it would add 1500 new campsites to provincial parks by the end of 1999. In both Canada and the United States camping is the second most popular recreational activity (hiking is the first). Camping is a Canadian tradition, enthusiastically adopted by new immigrants, visitors, and long-term residents alike. It provides access to some of the best scenery in the world. There really is no excuse not to give it a try.

Facilities Offered in B.C. Provincial Parks

National and provincial park campgrounds are well signposted on major highways. A sign 2 kilometres before the campground turnoff is the first warning campers receive, followed by another sign 400 metres from the campground. The second sign gives directions to the access road. If a campground is full or closed, the park operator will post notices on these roadside signs stating this fact.

*BC Parks road signpost (left) and
information board (right).*

At the campground entrance you will find an information board that displays a map of the campground along with a list of emergency telephone numbers, campground hazards, and neighbouring campgrounds. If the campground accepts reservations (see below), the location of reserved spots will be indicated at the entrance. Some campgrounds have information boards dotted around the park and on interpretative trails detailing the fauna, flora, or history of the region.

Your camping spot

One of the joys of arriving at a BC Parks campground is the anticipation of finding the perfect spot in which to establish camp. Will it overlook the river or lake? Will it have access to the beach, be surrounded by cottonwood trees, and have fantastic views? Or will it be more like a parking space, with no outlook other than the two huge RVs you are forced in between? The provincial park campgrounds in this book have been selected because they offer superior camping spots. All sites, regardless of size, will have a fire pit (as long as the region does not have a long-term ban on campfires), a picnic table, and a post at the entrance where the BC Parks representative puts your receipt and which tells if the space is reserved. Some parks have "double spots" ideal for two-family camping. Larger campgrounds also have "pull-thrus" designed for the largest RV. Like the best hotel chambermaids, BC Parks staff regularly rake and tidy these campsites, remove any garbage, and neatly stack the unused firewood.

If you are travelling with a pet, please note that pets are allowed in B.C. parks as long as they are on a leash. Some parks have designated areas specifically for dogs. Dogs are forbidden on beaches unless the park has a designated "dog beach."

Washrooms/Showers

The biggest reason why a large percentage of the population is resistant to camping is undoubtedly related to misconceptions concerning "going" outside. Since I spent the first thirty years of my life in Europe, where finding toilet tissue in the washroom of a downtown pub after 8:00 p.m. is a luxury, the proposition that BC Parks washroom facilities are unpleasant amazes me. I admit a pit toilet in a popular provincial park in the heat of July may not be the place to retreat with your favourite novel, but you can be assured that despite the slightly unpleasant odours and the flies that swarm to greet you as you open the door, it will have been cleaned within the last twelve hours and there will be copious quantities of toilet tissue (single-ply however). Remember there is always more than one pit toilet at a site, and some in the less busy areas of the campground have not been used as much as others, so may not suffer from the same odours.

There are basically three types of toilets in BC Parks. The first are the pit toilets—"thunderboxes"— wooden boxes painted white and divided along gender lines. Naturally these are the ones that cause the most concern. I have found that by and large they are only smelly at certain times of the year (and even then they're not too odoriferous), always lock, and are perfectly adequate. On a visit to BC Parks head office in Victoria I found ten pages of specifications on how these thunderboxes should be positioned, constructed, painted, ventilated, etc. Some BC Parks official

A typical "thunderbox" in a B.C. park.

obviously put a lot of time and effort into designing these places, so think twice before criticizing them.

The second type of toilet facility looks like a thunderbox but houses an odour-free flushing toilet. These are not equipped with sinks. The third type is the conventional washroom facility with sinks, which may or may not contain showers. BC Parks staff clean and service all three types of facilities twice daily.

The larger washrooms have mirrors that almost without exception give a distorted, unclear image, so do not expect to be able to apply make-up in front of one. The temperatures in some campground showers may be a bit erratic, but they are generally adequate and, unlike those in many private campgrounds, do not cut off after you have had the allotted two minutes and still have shampoo in your hair. Some campgrounds have family shower rooms and baby change facilities.

Fires

Each year visitors to BC Parks campgrounds burn the equivalent of 2000 logging-truck loads of wood, a quantity equal to 235 hectares of forest. BC Parks is attempting to reduce the consumption of wood and suggests the following options: burn logs made of wax and cardboard; have a campfire every second night; build small fires; share a fire. As well, the campground fire situation is currently under review by BC Parks. In the past, free wood was available in each BC Parks campground, and in some campgrounds wood was delivered to your spot. In 1998 fifteen parks implemented a fee, selling wood for five dollars a bundle. This practice could be extended in 1999.

Fires are permitted only in the fire pit of the camping spot and only when there is not a fire ban, which may occur at the height of summer

A woodpile at a BC Parks campsite.

*Getting water at a campsite can be reminiscent
of the way our ancestors collected water.*

when it's hot and dry. The information board at the park entrance will indicate if there is a fire ban, and often all firewood will be removed from the park to ensure this rule is observed.

Water

Water is available either from a conventional water faucet or from a pump. Collecting water from a pump is a bit of an art (expect to get wet feet) and in certain parks will give your arm muscles a good workout. You may want to include a funnel with your camping gear as it can help considerably when you are collecting pump water.

Garbage/Recycling

You can always tell when a campground is in an area inhabited by bears by the situation of the garbage bins. If they are swinging barrels or elongated metal cylinders with tight lids and a catch, you can be sure there are bears around. If they are like the garbage bins you find at home, there are not. BC Parks recycles, although the extent of recycling varies between parks. Garbage depositors (often located near the woodpile) are regularly emptied to discourage animals. Remember that you should never leave garbage at your campsite as it attracts racoons, chipmunks, skunks, crows, and even bears. I remember vividly the night we retired to our tent a little the worse for the litre of wine we had consumed with dinner, only to be wakened at 1:30 a.m. by the sound of wild creatures ripping through our belongings. Racoons had discovered our garbage, which we had neglected to take to the bins, and in the early hours were having their own noisy picnic. From where we were lying in the tent, these animals sounded more like huge moose than little racoons. Now no matter how mellow we feel, we always remember to dispose of the garbage.

A note on bears: B.C. is bear country, with a quarter of the black bears and half the grizzlies in Canada. Campers should never approach or feed bears.

Food-conditioned bears—those that scavenge food from garbage cans and picnic tables—begin to associate food with people, lose their natural fear of humans, and become a threat to campers and to themselves. With caution and sensible behaviour, bear country can be safely camped and enjoyed. (You can find further detailed information on bears in a book by David Smith entitled *Backcountry Bear Basics*.)

During a visit to Wells Gray Provincial Park in the summer of 1998 I was fascinated to read details of bear sightings near the popular Clearwater Campground where we were camped. I noted that the most recent had been three days before our arrival, at campsite number 28. As we were at site number 12 I felt quite safe. The following morning I awoke to find a huge pile of bear scat at the entrance to our site. This had not been present when we arrived. A black bear had passed within feet of our tent during the night while we were asleep. This was a good reminder to us to exercise caution and be aware of this very real hazard.

A BC Parks amphitheatre—bring a pillow to sit on, and maybe a blanket, the seats are hard and the evenings can be cool.

Plan a picnic and take your kids to the playground provided at many campsites.

Recreational activities

Activities offered vary of course, depending on the size and location of the park. Many parks have boat launches, safe swimming areas (but no lifeguards), hiking trails, adventure playgrounds for children, horseshoe pits, volleyball nets, large grassy areas for ball games, and amphitheatres for evening programs.

Interpretative programs are offered in the larger B.C. parks throughout the summer months (usually at weekends). BC Parks staff or invited guests give these programs. Topics can range from information on wildlife and birds, including butterflies and moths, bats, snakes, and reptiles, to flowers, trees, and the night sky. The bear talks are always popular and include just as many stories from the audience as they do from the presenters. Talks usually last about an hour and take place outside, with the audience seated on hard wooden benches, so remember to bring your own chair or cushion. As the evening progresses, you may find you need bug repellent and a blanket. Interpretative programs are geared towards every age group and often draw on the expertise of the audience as well as the BC Parks presenter.

In 1984 BC Parks started the **Jerry Rangers Program**, the aim of which was to create in children "an understanding of conservation issues and knowledge of the natural and cultural environment as they relate to the provincial park system." A child joins by obtaining a Jerry Rangers Certificate from a representative of BC Parks and by promising to take care of the park by observing a number of rules outlined on the back of the certificate. Members can then take part in a wide variety of games, skits, crafts, and activities to earn Jerry Rangers stickers like the Nature Nut sticker (where participants learn of the park's natural history), the Dogged Detective sticker (which develops investigative skills to unravel park mysteries), the Safety Sense sticker (which promotes safety skills for

BC Parks operator at Tyhee Lake.

hiking, boating, and swimming), and the Earth Explorer sticker (an introduction to orienteering and survival skills). Programs are geared to the environment of each individual park and have names such as "Slippery Slimy Slugs," "The Bear Facts," and "Just Squidding Around." These activities occur twice daily in the larger parks during the summer months and are a great way for kids to make friends in a fun, educational environment. An adult must accompany any children attending these programs.

Look for campground hosts. They offer a wealth of information both in printed form and in conversation.

BC Parks Staff

BC Parks staff are delightful characters with unique personalities and idiosyncrasies. As the people responsible for these "huge open air hotels," as one described them, their job is to keep the washrooms clean and tidy, garbage cleared, woodpile stocked, and campsites clean; to collect fees; and of course to ensure we all remain happy campers. What a lovely task.· They wear blue shirts and shorts/trousers (brown in national parks) and are frequently an unbeatable source of information about the surrounding areas. They can also be useful in, for example, helping the novice camper light a campfire or suggesting the best place to pitch a tent.

In addition to salaried BC Parks staff, some campgrounds have **campground hosts**. These are people, usually retired, who volunteer to spend a month or more in a campground to offer advice and information to tourists. Their camping spots are easily recognizable as they have most of the comforts of home (artificial grass, potted plants, hanging baskets, awnings, flowers on the picnic table, welcome mat at the door of the RV, etc., etc.). A sign by their camping spot tells other campers when they are on duty. Campground hosts often tour the campground to check if visitors need anything, to ensure they are enjoying the facilities offered, and to give out BC Parks buttons, bumper stickers, and information leaflets.

Fees and Reservations

A fee of $8 to $18.50 (1999 prices) is charged for camping in B.C. provincial parks. The fee for national parks is $16 to $24, plus a charge for wood. The price variation depends on the facilities offered, with the most expensive campgrounds having showers. During the early evening hours a BC Parks representative will visit your campsite to collect the fee (cash only). You can pay for up to fourteen nights in any one location, although some of the most popular campsites may have a policy restricting your stay to seven nights. Fees are collected from April until October. Residents of B.C. over the age of 65 camp for half price before June 15 and after Labour Day (first Monday in September). Depending on their location, most provincial parks are open from April until October. The campgrounds in the two national parks (Yoho and Kootenay) detailed in this book have shorter operating periods.

In 1996 for the first time, patrons of BC Parks were able to reserve spaces in certain campgrounds. Now over three years old, the reservation process administered by "Discover Camping" is an immense success, with many thousands of people using it each year. In 1999 over 60 campgrounds accepted reservations.

To reserve a camping spot, campers call a toll-free number 1-800-689-9025 (in Greater Vancouver call 689-9025). Agents from Discover Camping take reservations seven days a week, from 7:00 a.m. to 7:00 p.m.

Campgrounds in this book that accept reservations

Barkerville	Moberly Lake
Bear Creek	Mount Robson
Blanket Creek	Okanagan Lake
Crooked River	Otter Lake
Ellison	Paarens Beach
Fintry	Premier Lake
Haynes Point	Shuswap Lake
Kikomun Creek	Syringa Creek
Kokanee Creek	Tyhee Lake
Lakelse Lake	Wasa Lake
Liard River Hotsprings	Wells Gray

Monday to Friday and from 9:00 a.m. to 5:00 p.m. Saturday and Sunday (Pacific time), from March 1 until September 15. Reservations can be made up to three months in advance and up to two days prior to arrival (five days for Liard River Hotsprings). Camping spots are available for reservation from March 15 to September 15. Specific campsites cannot be reserved, so one of the disadvantages of the service is you could find your allocated spot is not the most desirable one in the campground. Double sites can be requested if they are available. As mentioned above, the length of stay is limited to fourteen days per calendar year. When you make a reservation, you will be given a confirmation number, which you will need to quote if you have to make a change or cancellation. (You can change a reservation by phoning the number given above. Changes and cancellations must be made two days prior to arrival—five days for the remote Liard River Hotsprings.) You may also be asked for the confirmation number upon arriving at the park.

At the time you make a reservation you will pay all fees for the reservation service and the campsite. (Discover Camping accepts Visa or Mastercard.) The reservation fee is $6.42 per night to a maximum of $19.26 (including GST) for three or more nights. If you decide to alter your reservation you will incur an additional fee of $6.42.

Those who wish to reserve a campsite during one of the three summer long weekends—Victoria Day (third weekend in May), BC Day (first weekend in August), or Labour Day (first weekend in September)—must book a minimum of three nights—Friday, Saturday, Sunday.

As previously mentioned, the Discover Camping Reservation system has been extremely successful, sometimes with all reservable spaces in the most popular campgrounds booked for weekends through the summer by the end of April. Some parks contain more than one campground and not all campgrounds accept reservations. All parks have some spaces allocated on a first come, first served basis, although the percentage of non-reservable space can be as low as 20 percent. I have found that in all but the most popular parks (i.e., Okanagan Lake, Haynes Point) reservations are not necessary for weekdays in the months of April, May, June, and September.

For more information see the Discover Camping internet site at http://www.discovercamping.ca.

Defining the Best

The provincial and national parks I have chosen to include in this text offer a wide range of activities both within their immediate environment and beyond, have good facilities, and have been identified by myself and others as excellent places to spend more than one night. While there are a number of outstanding private camping facilities, I considered only BC Parks and Canadian Parks Service sites, though the final chapter does offer guidance on camping in British Columbia Forestry Service (BCFS) sites for those who want to experience rustic wilderness camping.

It is inevitable that in defining the best I show my own personal preferences. I do not fish but adore hiking, and no doubt if I were an angler I would have included a few more fishing hot spots at the expense of some hiking locations. Likewise, my ideal camping location is away from a major centre of population, although many campers, especially those with children, often wish to be near a town. In deciding what to include I considered statistics from BC Parks that indicate the most popular parks in the province. During the last seven years I have camped in over 100 provincial park campgrounds and visited more than 140. By combining my own experience with the research data, I have selected over 40 campgrounds in northern, central, and southeastern B.C. that offer truly fantastic camping adventures.

How to Use This Book

In an attempt to cover a broad range of camping preferences, I have included government-run campgrounds with the most comprehensive provisions alongside those with the most basic. The selected campgrounds are divided into eight chapters. Each chapter focusses on the best campgrounds in a particular category—the best campgrounds for families, at the lakeside, for hiking, with hot springs, for adventure, and for kissing, as well as hidden gem and forestry campgrounds. At the end of each chapter I have recommended other campgrounds that may also be regarded as "the best" in these categories. I've indicated their location using Tourism BC's regional designations (i.e, High Country, Rockies). In the appendix I

Camping Etiquette

While few formal rules exist, there is a definite camping etiquette that should be observed for the benefit of all. Most points on the list below serve only as a gentle reminder of common sense.

1. Quiet time is from 10:00 p.m. to 7:00 a.m. In all my years of camping I have never been disturbed by fellow campers during these times (racoons, elk, owls, deer, trains, and strong winds have disturbed my slumber, but never people). Provincial and national parks close their gates between 11:00 p.m. and 7:00 a.m. to prevent late arrivals and visitors from disturbing the peace.

2. At certain times of the year the threat of forest fires is immense and may result in a ban on campfires. Check park information boards to determine status. At all times, light fires only in metal fire pits and take heed of notices about the potential fire hazards.

3. Store food in your vehicle, in airtight containers, and away from animals. If you do not have a vehicle and are in an area frequented by bears, hang food in bags suspended well out on a tree branch, at least four metres above the ground. With between 120,000 and 160,000 black bears in B.C., this is not a rule to ignore.

4. To protect the vegetation, camp only in designated areas.

5. Reduce waste and recycle as much as possible. BC Parks provides dispensers for recycling; use them.

6. Take only as much from the woodpile as you need. One of the many advantages B.C. provincial parks have over national park, private, and American campgrounds is that firewood is provided at no charge (though this may change in the future). Wood should not be wasted.

7. Checkout time is 11:00 a.m. and the maximum length of stay is fourteen days per year in any one park. A camping party is regarded as a family from the same address or a maximum of four people thirteen years or older, of which one must be over the age of sixteen.

8. Cutting branches and picking flowers, berries, or mushrooms is prohibited in provincial and national parks. Enjoy the natural flora and fauna by looking, smelling, or photographing, but leave it as you found it for others to have the same pleasure.

9. Clean your campsite on departure, making sure all food remains and garbage have been cleared away.

10. Keep pets on a leash in campgrounds and all other restricted areas.

11. Do not use your fire pit as a handy garbage disposal unit. Partly burned food will tempt wildlife, and blackened cans are an annoyance to whoever follows.

12. BC Parks literature states that only one camping vehicle is allowed on a campsite. This vehicle must fit comfortably without damaging the location or causing a nuisance to other campers. The only exceptions to this rule are when an additional vehicle is being towed or when group members arrive from a common home address in a separate vehicle. (The commuter vehicle must be registered at the same address as the registered party.)

13. Do not take powerboats near swimmers. Try to avoid disturbing the tranquillity of those enjoying the beach by revving engines excessively.

14. Alcohol is not permitted in the public areas of BC Parks but *is* allowed on your camping spot.

provide addresses where you can obtain more information to supplement your enjoyment of B.C.

Each campground entry contains a number of subheadings. After the introduction, which justifies why the campground is included as one of the best in the category, "History" gives a synopsis of the area's past. "Location" tells how to find the campground and describes its geographical features. "Facilities" lists the number of camping spots and the services (i.e., showers, toilets, wood, water, reservations, etc.). "Recreational activities" outlines what opportunities, if any, the campground offers for hiking, cycling, fishing, boating, wildlife viewing, and family activities, as well as what attractions are available in the surrounding area. Finally, "Summary" gives some personal or anecdotal information about the campground. Numerous photographs have also been included, and maps on page 22 show the location of each campground.

Camping Tips

One of the joys of camping is learning the little tricks that make it easier. Here are a few tips:

1. If the campground does not have a shower, leave a full plastic water container in the sun all day long and wash in warm water in the evening.
2. Take a water container and a funnel to collect water from the pump.
3. Carry a small amount of dry wood to make it easy to start a fire.
4. Cook vegetables (e.g. mushrooms, tomatoes, zucchini, peppers, and onions) by wrapping them in aluminium foil, sealing them in with spices.
5. If you do not have a reservation, try to arrive at a campground before 5:00 p.m., as the most popular hours for arrival are between 5:00 p.m. and 8:00 p.m.
6. It's a good idea to keep a keyring-size flashlight in your pocket for emergencies and for nightly excursions to the washroom.
7. Axes, matches, dry paper, plastic bags, rope, flashlights, candles, and aluminium foil are all camping basics. Add toilet paper to that list if you are camping in BCFS sites.
8. Spread a tarp under the tent for extra protection against the damp.
9. Keep one set of clothes specifically for wearing by the campfire so you have only one outfit smelling of wood smoke.
10. Dry wet wood by propping logs against the fire pit.

Now you are ready for a camping adventure...GO FOR IT!

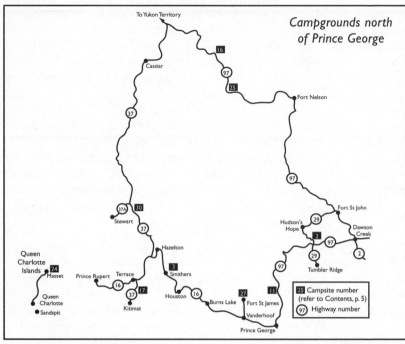

Campgrounds north
of Prince George

To Yukon Territory

Cassiar

16

97

25

Fort Nelson

37

97

97A 30

Stewart

37

Fort St John

29

Hudson's
Hope

Dawson
Creek

2

97

2

Hazelton

29

97

Tumbler Ridge

Queen
Charlotte
Islands   24
Masset

Prince Rupert   Terrace

16   37   17

3   Smithers

Houston   16   Burns Lake   27   Fort St James   11

Kitimat

Queen
Charlotte
Sandspit

Vanderhoof

Prince George

25 Campsite number
(refer to Contents, p. 5)
97 Highway number

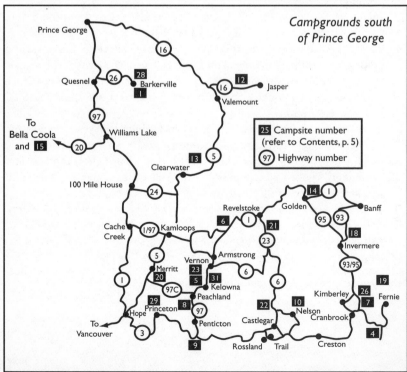

Campgrounds south
of Prince George

Prince George

16

Quesnel   26   28

Barkerville

1

16   12

Valemount   Jasper

97

25 Campsite number
(refer to Contents, p. 5)
97 Highway number

To
Bella Coola
and   15   20

Williams Lake

13   5

Clearwater

100 Mile House   24

14   1

Golden   Banff

Revelstoke   95   93

Cache
Creek   1/97   Kamloops   6   1   21

23

5

Merritt   Vernon   23   6   18

20   5   Invermere

1   97C   Kelowna   6   93/95

Peachland   19

29   8   22   10   Kimberley   26

Princeton   97   Nelson   7   Fernie

To
Vancouver   Hope   Penticton   Castlegar   Cranbrook

3   Rossland   Trail   Creston   4

9

THE BEST FAMILY CAMPGROUNDS

In many respects the Best Family Campgrounds have attributes similar to the Best Lakeside Campgrounds (Chapter 2). With the exception of Barkerville, all have access to fresh water and therefore are a delight for children. In selecting my preferences for families I have attempted to choose campgrounds in different areas of the province that are large, accept reservations, and for the most part have all facilities including showers, flush toilets, and disabled access.

Barkerville is in the Cariboo area of B.C. and although it does not offer waterfront activities, it does grant access to a reconstructed historical town, fun for every age group. Moberly Lake is probably one of the most remote family-oriented campgrounds, found in the Peace River region of the province. I selected it because of the numerous attractions not only within its boundaries, but also in the surrounding area. I like Tyhee Lake on the Yellowhead Highway because it is a relatively small campground (59 spaces) that, because of its size, seems to foster family friendships. This, together with 200 metres of beach and every camping convenience, makes it a popular choice. I describe Kikomun Creek, my fourth choice, as similar to an English country estate because of its size. It is situated in the southern Rockies, and you can spend weeks here exploring the many trails, swimming in the lakes, cycling, or fishing. Finally, Bear Creek has access to Okanagan Lake and this fact, coupled with its easy accessibility to major population centres, makes it a great family vacation spot.

All these campgrounds are very popular; if you are planning a trip in July or August be sure to invest in a reservation to avoid disappointment.

1. Barkerville

This is a fun place to stay, steeped in the history of gold mining and prospecting. Barkerville Provincial Park is within walking distance of the authentically reconstructed historical site of Barkerville, a gold-rush town that was once the largest settlement west of Chicago and north of San Francisco. The town of Barkerville is not part of the 457-hectare provincial park and is administered by a different arm of the provincial government than the park, but it is adjacent.

History

The community of Barkerville developed as a result of the Cariboo Gold Rush of the 1860s. In 1862 an English prospector named Billy Barker found gold, and within

Jayne poses at the Barkerville signpost.

48 hours he and his friends mined $1000 worth, thereby ensuring that Barkerville was firmly established on the gold-rush map. The following years saw hundreds of prospectors travel to the region to stake claims, and the town of Barkerville grew. On September 16, 1868, disaster struck. Barkerville was completely destroyed by a fire that broke out in a small room adjoining Barry and Adler's saloon. In the space of 90 minutes the town was burnt to the ground. It was quickly rebuilt and by 1871 growth had peaked and was beginning to decline. By 1900 Barkerville was only a shadow of its former self, although it remained a supply centre for Cariboo gold fields in the 1930s. In 1957 the provincial government decided to restore Barkerville as a historical park as part of its contribution to the province's 1958 centennial. In doing so it gave the people of the province and tourists a window on times gone by. The provincial park was established in 1959.

Location

One of the joys of Barkerville is simply getting there along the history-laden highway that leads to it. The park is 89 kilometres east of Quesnel

Cottonwood House—step back in time on your way to historic Barkerville.

on Highway 26. It is easy to imagine prospectors travelling this road by stagecoach or with pack horses on the last leg of their journey to find gold. Numerous stops of interest are signposted along the way, including Cottonwood House (see below), one of the oldest residences in the province, and Lovers Leap, where an amorous stagecoach driver fell in love with one of his passengers, proposed marriage, and said if she refused he would drive his stagecoach over her. According to the legend the damsel declined, but fortunately for her a gallant hero in the guise of a fellow passenger persuaded the lovesick driver to complete the trip. Other stops of interest tell tales of murders and hangings. The provincial park is located 2 kilometres from the community of Wells, which has shops, accommodation, gas, restaurants, and a post office.

Facilities

BC Parks administers three campgrounds—Forest Rose, Lowhee, and Government Hill—within this provincial park, with a total of 168 spots and group camping. Forest Rose has pull-through sites, and both Forest Rose and Lowhee have showers. Lowhee Campground is the largest, with 87 sites, including 50 available for reservation. It also has the best facilities including sani-station, children's play area, telephone, and information centre. Forest Rose is farthest from the town of Barkerville but is the quietest (56 sites) and is my personal preference, although you have to drive over unsightly open-pit mine workings to get to it. Government Hill has only 25 sites, with some small, unappealing, closely packed camping spots and only basic facilities. The park is wheelchair accessible. The small Grubstake Store is located between the Lowhee and Forest Rose Campgrounds.

Recreational activities

Hiking

There are several hiking trails in the area ranging from short walks to day hikes. Trail maps can be obtained from the Barkerville Administration Centre. Two of the most popular trails climbing to Murray Ridge are the Yellowhawk and Jubilee Trails. You can pick up Yellowhawk 3 kilometres along Bowron Lake Road. It is 8.4 kilometres long. The Jubilee Trail is located 5 kilometres along the same road and is 9.4 kilometres long. Both trails are well marked, with elevation gains of just over 600 metres.

Fishing/Boating

Jack of Clubs Lake, which you drive by on the way to Wells, has fishing and boating potential.

Gold panning

Everyone should try gold panning when they visit the area. You can buy a gold pan at the Grubstake Store, but I found pans to be more reasonably priced in Wells. Novices can get an introduction to gold panning at the Barkerville historic site, where lively and entertaining instructors tell how it should be done. Be advised that there is definitely still gold to be found in "them thar hills." In 1991 an eight-ounce nugget worth over $10,000 was found in Gold Panners Park, just outside Wells. Try not to get too smitten with the pursuit, as staking a claim can cost anywhere from $5000 to $15,000. (*Goldpanning in the Cariboo* by Jim Lewis and Charles Hart, published by Heritage House, is a useful guide to gold panning and gold creeks in the Cariboo region.)

Family activities

Of course the biggest attraction here is the town of Barkerville, with over 100 displays of living history and more than 40 buildings dating back to the nineteenth century. The town has bakeries, hotels, restaurants, a theatre, a courthouse, churches, shops, and offices, all staffed by guides in period costumes who are happy to answer questions. Tours are conducted on a regular basis, and shows are put on in the theatre. There is even a tour of the cemetery conducted by a sombre-faced minister. Street theatre is often the order of the day. When we visited there was a hose carriage race between two fire departments and a march by the Women's Temperance League. These ever-changing activities ensure that the tourist can easily spend one or two days exploring the past. Barkerville is now one of the most popular tourist attractions in the province, with over 100,000 visitors a year. It appeals to every age group.

Cemetery at Barkerville—what stories it could tell!

Activities adjacent to the park

Wells is a pleasant community to wander through, with many interesting, recently restored buildings. Tour operators from Wells run canoe and kayaking trips on the nearby Bowron Lake circuit, which is regarded as one of the top ten canoe circuits in the world (see Chapter 7). The start of the circuit is 23 kilometres along a good gravel road from Wells. It's worth taking this drive just to see the snow-covered peaks of the Cariboo Mountains reflected in the waters of Bowron Lake.

Cottonwood House, 60 kilometres from Wells, offered accommodation to the gold-rush travellers from 1865 until the 1900s. Today it is a historical monument, a lovely, reasonably priced ($2.00 per adult) place to visit, with a quaint bakery, small farm, stagecoach rides, and numerous wooden buildings.

Summary

Barkerville is a fascinating place, suitable for every age group. It is one of the best examples of B.C. history and should be on everyone's list of places to go. The camping experience is, however, secondary to visiting the town. This is not a campground I imagine many coming to for a week at a time, as it is busy and does not have the draw of a nearby lake, stream, or ocean to relax beside. It is a place to learn about times gone by and to dream of gold. I have to confess that although I had planned to camp here one September, the inclement weather steered me towards the newly renovated Wells Hotel, which had a crackling fire, lounge, licensed dining room, and extremely comfy beds. It also served a fantastic breakfast. Even the most dedicated camper deserves some luxury from time to time.

2. Moberly Lake

This is very much a family vacation spot, but that should not put off those without children. Although when I visited, children outnumbered adults in a ratio of what seemed like 100 to 1, a number of other campers who were clearly in their golden years were also having fun watching the youngsters and enjoying the facilities the park offers. Even though it is one of the most popular campgrounds in the Peace-Liard region, its northern location means accommodation is usually readily available, and the individual campsites are wonderful.

History

Moberly Lake is named after Henry John Moberly, a trader and trapper who worked for the Hudson's Bay Company and who was reputed to be the first white man to discover the lake, in 1865. He settled on the north shores of the lake in the mid-1800s. Cree people moved to the area after the Riel Rebellion of 1885. Now the town has a population of less than 300.

Location

The provincial park created in 1966 covers 98 hectares of land on the south shore of Moberly Lake in the Moberly River Valley between the Rocky Mountain foothills to the west and the Great Plains to the east. It is set amongst a dense forest of white spruce, aspen, and poplar, with large cottonwood trees dominating the lower lying areas. The park is accessed by turning off Highway 29, 24 kilometres northeast of Chetwynd, and taking a good gravel road for 3 kilometres. All services are available at Chetwynd, with more limited ones available 11 kilometres away at the community of Moberly Lake.

Facilities

The 109 large, private camping spots set in a forest of mature white spruce and aspen make this a desirable destination. Streams, ideal for cooling cans of drinks, flow through the campground itself, and a few sites overlook the lake. Grassy sites are available and there is ample space for the longest RV. The park is accessible to the disabled. There is a sani-station but only pit toilets and no showers. Reservations are accepted.

Recreational activities

Hiking

A number of small hiking trails, including self-guided nature trails, meander through the park. None are that arduous, making them appropriate for any age group. Trails by the lake lead through the cottonwood trees, which at certain times of the year give off a heady aroma, enjoyable for everyone except those with hay fever.

Fishing

The lake has northern pike, Dolly Varden, lake whitefish, and char, and a marina adjacent to the park supplies all the gear needed for what has been described as a productive water by those who know.

Boating

There is a boat launch in the park, and powerboats are permitted on the lake. When I visited, the jet-ski brigade was not out, so a tranquil time was had.

Wildlife viewing

Due to the abundance of berries growing in the area, bears, as well as people and moose, are frequent visitors. However, it is the smaller creatures such as red squirrels, beavers, and rabbits that you are more likely to see. More than twenty species of birds including bald eagles, American kestrels, belted kingfishers, and herring gulls have been recorded within the park's boundary.

Family activities

With over 300 kilometres of beach, this is a location for taking in the rays. Sunbathing, picnicking, and swimming are all possible activities if the weather is accommodating. There is an adventure playground in the park and a picnic shelter and change house located near the beach. During the peak summer months BC Parks provides interpretative programs for both adults and children.

Activities adjacent to the park

One of the benefits of Moberly Lake is that if the weather is inclement there is plenty to do in the surrounding region. There is a marina and a golf course within walking distance of the park, while the towns of Chetwynd to the south and Hudson's Hope to the north offer a range of recreational activities. Both towns have tourist information offices where you can pick up maps and information. Chetwynd has a number of huge chainsaw sculptures of birds and animals by B.C. artists, a heritage museum, and a trapper's cabin you can visit. The Old Baldy Hiking Trail, which offers awe-inspiring views of the valley, has recently been developed and is great whatever the season. If the weather is truly awful, check out Chetwynd's leisure centre with its brilliant wave pool, said to be one of the best in the region.

To the north, Hudson's Hope on the banks of the Peace River has a museum that documents the early trapping and coal-mining industries of the area, but its true draw is the W.A.C. Bennett Dam, one of the largest earth-filled dams in the world. This edifice, a twenty-minute drive from the town, is spectacular. There are free underground tours of the dam, as well as a number of hands-on exhibits for kids, information films, interpretative programs, a visitors centre, and a restaurant. The picnic area outside the dam has great views of the lake. The entire complex is fascinating and educational. Pack a picnic and expect to spend the best part of a day to really appreciate it.

Summary

One of the biggest draws of this campground is that it provides activities both within its boundaries and in the two adjacent communities, so it is possible to plan a week's vacation here without being too concerned if the weather is not great. Sunsets over the lake are awesome, so remember to bring the camera. This campground tends not to be crowded, thanks to its northern location, and yet it has facilities and scenery that rival some of the most popular provincial parks in the province.

*Views of the W.A.C. Bennett Dam, one of the
largest earth-filled dams in the world.*

3. Tyhee Lake

I have only stayed here once but have visited on numerous occasions to enjoy the picnicking opportunities the location offers anyone travelling the Yellowhead Highway through picturesque Bulkley Valley. With only 59 camping spots, this campground never feels crowded even when it is full, so it offers a quieter camping experience compared to campgrounds with over 100 spaces. It is a friendly, welcoming site where visitors have the time and inclination to stop and chat with no pressures from the outside world. Expect to make some good friends if your plans include more than a couple of nights at Tyhee.

History

The Bulkley River is named after Colonel Charles S. Bulkley, who in 1864 was given the task by the Collins Overland Telegraph Co. of constructing a telegraph line across B.C. to Alaska. This line would then connect with a line from Russia via Siberia. The project was abandoned in 1867 when the Trans-Atlantic cable was successfully completed. Despite this disappointment, Bulkley's presence in the area was not without some benefit, as the Kispiox people managed to salvage enough discarded wire from the project to build a suspension bridge across the Bulkley River. The lake that gives its name to the campground was originally called Maclure Lake after one of the Collins Overland Telegraph Co. surveyors, but the name was later changed to Tyhee, which means "fish" in the Gitksan language.

At the southwest end of Tyhee Lake are the remains of the town of Aldermere (now on private land), which developed in the 1800s. At one time this community had a hotel, stables, and a post office and rivalled the

The Bulkley and Telkwa Rivers meet at Telkwa.

communities of Smithers and Telkwa, but it started to die when the telegraph line was abandoned, and by 1915 little remained.

Location

The 33-hectare park lies on the banks of Tyhee Lake in the Bulkley River Valley on the Nechako Plateau. To the east lies the Babine Range of the Skeena Mountains and to the west the Telkwa and Bulkley Ranges of the Hazelton Mountains. Look for glaciers on these mountains when you are driving to and from the campground. The town of Smithers is a fifteen-minute drive from the campground, while the nearer picture-postcard community of Telkwa, 2 kilometres east of the park, offers food, gas, and accommodation.

Facilities

All 59 camping spots are located in a second-growth forest of trembling aspen. The original forest was destroyed by fire 50 years ago, so the foliage is not dense, but all spaces are private and secluded and can accommodate every type of vehicle. There are also a number of sites specifically for tenters. Tyhee has all amenities including a sani-station, showers (at the beach), flush toilets, and disabled access, and it accepts reservations.

Recreational activities

Hiking

A number of small trails lead through the park, connecting the campground with the beach area. The 2.5-kilometre Aldermere Trail leads along the shoreline to a marsh-viewing platform where at the right times of the day there are opportunities to see a variety of birds and mammals (see below).

Fishing

The lake yields cutthroat trout and stocked rainbow trout. I have been informed that younger anglers may wish to try their luck and fish for minnows like peamouth chub, red shiner, and pygmy whitefish (good luck in trying to identify them!). For the serious angler, pools near Telkwa contain salmon and steelhead.

Boating

Powerboats are permitted on the lake, and a concrete boat launch is available near the day-use area.

Wildlife viewing

As mentioned above, a viewing platform located by the boat launch provides opportunities to see a number of mammals, birds, reptiles, and insects. The dead trees and bulrushes provide habitat for birds such as the downy woodpecker and red-winged blackbird, while loons, ruffed grouse, red-

The marsh-viewing platform at Tyhee Lake Campground.

necked grebes, and an array of songbirds inhabit the lakeshore. Early morning and dusk are the best times to see these birds. Mammals include beavers, squirrels, black bears, and moose, the latter rarely seen in the park itself.

Family activities

Over 200 kilometres of sandy beach is the number one attraction in this park. Children and adults adore swimming in the clear, reed-free waters, and there are picnicking and sunbathing opportunities both on the beach and on a grassed area close by. Additional facilities include an adventure playground, a horseshoe pitch, volleyball nets, a covered log picnic shelter, and the quiet roads of the campground that offer biking routes for cyclists of every age. BC Parks staff give numerous interpretative programs during the summer months and advertise these on the doors of the pit toilets. When I stayed they included "Faunal Pursuits," a quiz about animals; "Insectophilia," a lecture on our six-legged friends; as well as talks on climatology and plant identification, all in the space of three days!

Activities adjacent to the park

The lovely town of Telkwa, where the green Telkwa River meets the blue Bulkley, has a number of photogenic old buildings dating back to the early part of the twentieth century, together with a heritage museum. A visitors centre gives details of horseback riding and canoeing adventures in the vicinity, along with information on a walking tour of the community.

Tyhee Lake is a perfect spot for a bike ride.

Although I have not driven it, the Telkwa River Road is reputed to be a scenic drive from which you can see evidence of old mine workings. Farther west the larger town of Smithers nestles below the domineering 2621-metre Hudson Bay Mountain. It has a Germanic feel and a friendly, redbrick high street with numerous gift shops, cafes, and restaurants. The 1925 Central Park Building contains an art gallery and museum. Driftwood Canyon Provincial Park, northeast of Smithers, houses one of the world's most significant fossil beds, a fascinating place if you like rocks.

Summary

Tyhee Provincial Park is in the midst of a wonderful, unspoilt area of B.C., and due to its size it never feels crowded or rushed. Although for many the park is well located for a one-night stop en route between Prince George and Prince Rupert, its primary attraction must be for those campers who want to unwind over a number of days. It is perfect for stressed parents who want to spend time relaxing and bonding with their kids and for those who seek the less commercialized side of family camping in B.C. provincial parks.

4. Kikomun Creek

An excellent place for family camping if ever there was one. This campground feels to me like an English country estate with its large, open grasslands. A number of quiet, paved roads take you to locations in different regions of the park: the day-use area at Surveyors Lake, the main Surveyors Campground, the group camping area, South Pond Campground, the boat launch, and Kookanusa Reservoir. (BC Parks spells the reservoir's name "Kookanusa," but other guidebooks spell it "Koocanusa," claiming the name is a combination of Kootenay, Canada, and USA.) These different attractions and facilities are not closely packed together but are kilometres apart. The park consequently feels huge—much larger than its 682 hectares—just because you see so much of it as you go from place to place. This gives it quite a different feel compared to other provincial parks.

History

The park was established in 1972 to provide facilities for recreationalists as well as to preserve an example of Ponderosa pine/grassland habitat. The productive grasslands in and around the park were used initially by the Ktunaxa people who hunted deer, moose, mountain sheep, goats, geese, and grouse, and then by the European settlers who set up cattle ranches. The Ktunaxa people named the creek 'Qikmin, a name that referred to its tendency to dry up or shrink in the summer months. The construction of the Libby Dam in Montana created the huge reservoir.

South Pond Campground at Kikomun Creek.

Location

Kikomun Creek is situated in the southern region of the Rocky Mountain Trench, 68 kilometres from Cranbrook. Turn off Highway 3/93 at Elko, 32 kilometres west of Fernie, and take the paved road 11 kilometres south. Some services are available at Jaffray, 11 kilometres from the park, but the nearest are at a private marina 4 kilometres from the park's entrance. The marina supplies gas, propane, and fast foods, and has a food store.

Facilities

The quality of the camping spots offered in the three campgrounds varies tremendously. In my opinion, by far the best location is Surveyors Campground, a large campground with every amenity—including reservable spots, wheelchair accessibility, and showers—and spaces that can accommodate either the largest RV or smallest tent (tent pads available). Because of the sparse vegetation, many of these spaces feel quite open, but they are far enough apart to be completely private. This campground is on two levels, close to two sandy beaches, and has a volunteer host to provide information and advice.

The second campground is South Pond, which provides a regimented line of spaces with no privacy, although a large grassy area nearby invites you to pitch your tent. Only the basic amenities are offered here (pit toilets, wood, fire pit, picnic tables, water). This campground is close to the reservoir.

The third location is basically the parking lot near the boat launch, aptly named Boat Launch Campground, on Kookanusa Lake. Again only the basic facilities exist in this site, with little aesthetic offering. Choose this campground if boating is your primary passion. There is a sani-station at the main entrance to the park.

Recreational activities

Hiking

There are a number of easy hikes you can take here. Surveyors Lake Trail is an easy 45-minute walk around the lake. Hidden Lake is a shorter 30-minute interpretative stroll, while the Great Northern Rail Trail is a route for both mountain bikes and walkers (one to three hours depending on your mode of transportation, age, and level of fitness). Hikers of every age group can complete all trails. The first two feature interpretative boards along the route, while the latter is the subject of a leaflet you can collect from the campground host or at the start of the trail in Surveyors Campground.

Boat Launch Campground on Kookanusa Lake.

Cycling

The park is a delight to cycle in as there are not only quiet paved roads between the various campgrounds and day-use areas, but also a number of old roads and disused railway beds nearby. As mentioned above, the Great Northern Rail Trail is open to mountain bikers.

Fishing

The six lakes here—Surveyors, Hidden, Engineers, Skunk, Fisher, Muskrat, and Kookanusa—all have fishing opportunities. Kookanusa Lake is noted for kokanee, Rocky Mountain whitefish, cutthroat trout, and Dolly Varden, while smallmouth bass, eastern brook trout, and rainbow trout are more prevalent in the smaller lakes. During the fall, kokanee spawn in Kikomun Creek.

Boating

A concrete boat launch is provided at Kookanusa Lake. Powerboats are prohibited on the smaller lakes.

Wildlife viewing

The park is home to one of B.C.'s largest populations of western painted turtles, so called because of the bright pattern they exhibit underneath their shell. A wander around Surveyors Lake when the sun is out affords numerous opportunities to view these creatures soaking up the rays, while on a dull day their small faces can be seen bobbing in the water. Interpretative boards around the lake provide interesting facts about these cute reptiles.

Badgers, elk, black and grizzly bears, coyotes, cougars, and deer all inhabit the region. Birds seen in the park include osprey, mallards, red-tailed hawks, bald eagles, owls, and American kestrels.

Family activities

This is an ideal place to sojourn if you have children. There are two gorgeous sandy beaches by Surveyors Lake, and the waters of the lake are clear, clean, and quite warm. Young ones can spend hours building sandcastles, playing in the sunshine, or swimming to the offshore raft. There is an adventure playground near campsite 37 (Surveyors Campground). In the summer a whole host of programs are offered, including Jerry Rangers for the kids.

Activities adjacent to the park

Those who want to explore the local communities have many interesting options. The town of Fernie, a 40-minute drive from the park, has an interesting historical downtown core with buildings dating back to the 1890s. While in Fernie, take the historical walking tour, then visit the restored railway station for refreshments. Mount Fernie Provincial Park, 2 kilometres west of the town, is a good location for a picnic and walk. To the north of Kikomun is Fort Steele, which is well worth a visit whether you have children or not (see Wasa Lake Provincial Park in Chapter 2). Finally, the Kootenay Trout Hatchery on the Bull River, a 30-minute drive from the park, is a fascinating place to learn about the trout-rearing process.

Summary

I stayed here one hot weekday in early June when at 6:00 p.m. it was still warm enough to swim in the lake—which we had to ourselves, watched by a noisy osprey who had built a nest in a tree overlooking the waters. After dinner we returned to the waters to watch the sun go down in a blazing red sky, signifying that another perfect day was to follow. At this time the osprey's cries were accompanied by those of an owl and what at first we thought was the distant howl of a moose, but which turned out to be a motorcycle. We sat watching the waters as the moon rose and the stars came out. It was so bright we did not need the flashlights to light our way back to the tent. This is an outstanding provincial park, not only because of the facilities it offers, but also due to its location and the numerous activities close at hand.

5. Bear Creek

When I think of Bear Creek I am reminded of one of the most aromatic experiences of my life. I last visited in early spring, on a hot day when the smell of the cottonwood trees (which extend through the campground to the beach) was mingling with the scent of fir and pine to create an aroma that almost made me dizzy. Someone would make a fortune if they could bottle Bear Creek Bath Oil!

Smell is not the only draw here. In addition to its aromatic qualities, this is a campground with a friendly feel, ideal for families and campers who want the outdoors experience without travelling too far from the hustle and bustle of life. While Bear Creek is in the busy Okanagan region, it is situated on a relatively quiet road. Although the city of Kelowna is clearly in view, if you look the other way you can pretend it does not exist. Like the other campgrounds in the Okanagan, Bear Creek is extremely popular, so do not expect to find a spot easily in July or August, and consider reserving if you want a holiday here. Do consider visiting even if you do not have a reservation or an intention to camp, as it is a wonderful place for a picnic and walk.

History

The 167-hectare park was created in 1981. Prior to this the S.M. Simpson Company had owned the land, as the shoreline was ideal for "booming," or storing, floating logs. The Simpson Company sold its interest to Crown Zellerbach Canada Ltd., and in 1981 the Devonian Group of Alberta helped the B.C. government purchase the land. Crown Zellerbach retains the right to continue booming, so floating logs, an integral part of the B.C. economy, are often seen in the waters adjacent to the park (and a number

Bear Creek Campground looking over Okanagan Lake.

of "escaped" logs provide floating fun for children). The quality of the creek's water was recognized many years ago by the Kelowna Brewing Company, which established a brewery nearby. Unfortunately this is no longer in existence, although occasionally old quart beer bottles are found.

Location

Situated in the Central Okanagan Basin, Bear Creek (sometimes called Lambley Creek) is just 9 kilometres west of Kelowna on the western side of Okanagan Lake. You reach it via a paved access road. All services are available in Kelowna.

Facilities

The campground has 122 wonderful spots. Paved roads ribbon through the park, making access easy for even the largest RV. Some of the sites have

The "Steep and Deep Canyon."

views of the bubbling creek, so campers can sleep to the sound of singing waters. The campground is fully equipped with showers, flush and pit toilets, and access for the disabled. Reservations are accepted and strongly advised.

Recreational activities

Hiking

Although not long in distance (totalling only 10 kilometres), the hiking trails around Bear Creek are a delight. Information on the campground notice board states the main Canyon Rim Trail takes one to two hours to complete, although I did it in 40 minutes including stops for photographs of the lake, waterfalls, and gorge. It is quite steep in places but worth the effort, with many opportunities to photograph the rushing waters of Bear Creek. Interpretative boards along the route give information on the fauna and flora of the area, and if you are fortunate enough to take this trail in spring you will see and smell a stunning array of wildflowers. For those with less stamina the Mid Canyon Trail also grants access to some spectacular views, especially from the aptly named "Steep and Deep Canyon" lookout.

Boating–Fishing–Wildlife Viewing

Powerboats are permitted on the lake via the park boat launch. Anglers catch rainbow trout, kokanee, and whitefish.

Ornithologists are drawn to the hawks, owls, and swallows that live in the vicinity. In May you can hear tree frogs, while summer nights bring a chorus of crickets. In the early fall kokanee spawn in the lower waters of the creek. Rattlesnakes and gopher snakes that live in the area look similar, with the main difference being that rattlesnakes are poisonous. (I'd advise staying away from both of them!) There are illustrations on the information boards near the park change house, with the suggestion that you should travel to Kelowna hospital if you are bitten.

Family activities

This is a great place for children, with over 400 metres of sandy beach from which to enjoy the calm, safe waters. As mentioned above, the numerous washed-up logs enhance the range of activities to be undertaken in the lake. Millions (almost) of picnic tables are found in a large grassy area, and there is a change house, horseshoe pit, and adventure playground. The paved roads of the campground are cycling and rollerblading terrain. Small deposits of placer gold can be found in the creek, so remember to bring the gold pan and a lot of patience. Interpretative programs are given over the summer.

Activities adjacent to the park

The rapidly growing city of Kelowna (a name derived from the Okanagan First Nation word for grizzly bear) has a number of commercial activities including water parks, go-carts, paintball, an exotic butterfly garden, orchards with guided tours, golf courses, and of course wineries. Even if

Picnic tables galore.

the weather is bad, the park's proximity to Kelowna means there is always something to do. Fintry Provincial Park, north of Bear Creek, is also well worth a visit (see Chapter 5).

Summary

When travelling in this area, be sure to keep an eye out for the legendary Ogopogo, a lake serpent said to inhabit the waters. Native people call it N'xa'xa et kw, meaning "spiritually powerful in water." The best viewing spot is reported to be south of Bear Creek on the eastern side of the lake, 6 kilometres north of Okanagan Lake Provincial Park. It is believed B.C.'s answer to the Loch Ness Monster makes its home in an underwater cave in this region of the lake.

If there is no accommodation upon your arrival at Bear Creek, consider camping in one of B.C.'s newer parks, Fintry, 25 kilometres north of Bear Creek. When I visited Fintry it was still in its developmental stage, having opened in 1997, and consequently did not have the same "polished" feel as the other larger campgrounds of the Okanagan, including Bear Creek. In this respect it is quite rustic and charming. Fintry was the transportation hub for the Okanagan Valley, and a fleet of ferry boats operated from the wharf that is still on the site today. The wharf and numerous buildings and barns on the land are currently being restored. Fintry has a long shingle beach, access to the lake, and lots of country lanes and tracks to explore.

Additional Recommendations

The Best Lakeside Campgrounds See Chapter 2.

Lakelse See Chapter 4.

Fintry See Chapter 5.

Moyie Lake (Rockies) Although this is a popular beach and family camping location, the lake is somewhat crowded with powerboats. The campground has 104 spaces and all amenities.

Herald (High Country) On Shuswap Lake, this is a smaller version of Shuswap Lake Provincial Park (see Chapter 2), with 51 spaces and all amenities. Very popular.

Monck (High Country) Despite being somewhat sparse in vegetation, Monck offers a white, sandy beach and 71 camping spaces at a quiet location beside Nicola Lake.

Purden Lake (North by Northwest) For families in Prince George this is a convenient, 78-space campground with fantastic swimming and lake-related activities.

Beaumont (North by Northwest) First-rate swimming and fishing can be had at this 49-site location 130 kilometres west of Prince George.

THE BEST LAKESIDE CAMPGROUNDS

All the campgrounds in this section are on lakefront beaches (there is only one provincial park in the area covered by this book with an ocean shoreline. That is Naikoon, on the Queen Charlotte Islands—see Chapter 6). In many respects the sites in this chapter are also excellent locations for family camping, as many children adore water. Some of the six campgrounds featured offer commercialized provincial park camping (e.g., Shuswap, Wasa), while others provide a more out-of-the-way camping adventure (e.g., Crooked River).

Shuswap Lake has a long, white, sandy, lakeside beach in addition to being close to numerous commercial enterprises, so for those who seek a camping environment not too far from civilization, it is the place to be. Likewise, Wasa Lake Provincial Park has four beaches beside what is reputed to be one of the warmest lakes in the province, with all amenities close at hand. I have selected two campgrounds in the Okanagan. The first is Okanagan Lake, which boasts over 1000 metres of beach and two campgrounds; it is the most popular provincial park camping location in the Okanagan. Second, the much smaller but just as busy Haynes Point Provincial Park stretches along Okanagan Lake on a thin sandspit, and almost all sites have direct access to the beach. Kokanee Creek in the lovely Kootenay area of the province offers wonderful beaches and a fantastic array of wildflowers if you visit in June, or a breathtaking salmon-spawning spectacle for visitors in September. There's a lot to see and do both within the park and by travelling in the vicinity. Finally, Crooked River north of Prince George is a family-oriented, lakeside campground that does not suffer the same crowds as those in the Okanagan.

6. Shuswap Lake

If you are a camper who primarily enjoys hiking and exploring by land, and if you do not want to be surrounded by the younger generation, then you may decide that Shuswap is *not* the place to be as this provincial park and its environs are family oriented, dominated by lake- and beach-based activities. However, if you are a camper who loves the water or has little ones to entertain, this is your paradise. Shuswap Lake, with over 1000 kilometres of waterways that form an unconventional "H" shape, is a real magnet to the boating fraternity in the summer months. At the height of the season 350 houseboats, together with many hundreds of smaller craft, sail the warm waters. But it is not only boaters who flock to its shores. Those with young children are drawn by the kilometre of fine beach and the hot climate that guarantees many days can be lazily spent enjoying the sun, waters, and sand. And for those who just want to spend their time fishing, there is little to stop the pursuit of this pastime.

Shuswap Lake is actually made up of four arms: Shuswap Lake itself, Salmon Arm (including Mara Lake), Anstey Arm, and Seymour Arm, which all meet at Cinnemousun Narrows. The only disadvantage to this water wonderland is that it does get extremely busy, with the main campground operating at capacity in July and August (in 1997 there were 23,499 camping parties registered here). Fortunately there are a number of campgrounds accessible only by boat, so for those with alternative modes of transport, peace is only a few knots away.

History

Shuswap Lake Provincial Park was created in 1956 and is the largest and most commercialized park in the Shuswap region. The area is named after

Shuswap Lake has a kilometre of sandy beach and lots of sunshine.

Shuswap Lake campsite is in a dense second-growth forest.

the Shuswap people (Secwepemc First Nation), the most northern of the Salishan language group, who were the first to appreciate this extensive inland water system and to exploit the abundant natural resources. Evidence of these early inhabitants has been found in the form of kekulis— semi-underground pit houses built for enduring the winter—which have been found at Scotch Creek and Herald Provincial Park. Pictographs or rock paintings are also in evidence on rock faces around the lake. Europeans arrived throughout the nineteenth century as fur traders, explorers, and surveyors working for the Canadian Pacific Railway travelled the area. Gold was discovered in the region, which resulted in a flood of population. Towns and settlements rapidly appeared and disappeared as the gold prospectors arrived, worked the find, and moved on. Today little remains of their exploits.

Location

Shuswap Lake Provincial Park is situated on the lake from which it takes its name, on the old delta of Scotch Creek. The unusual lake formations are the result of glacial action that formed steep valley walls ringed by gently sloping mountainsides. The park is just under 150 hectares in area, which includes Copper Island, 2 kilometres off shore. Part of the reason for Shuswap's popularity is undoubtedly its central location, easily accessible from Highway 1. Ninety kilometres east of Kamloops, at Squilax, turn off the highway onto a 20-kilometre twisting, paved road that leads to the campground. Most supplies can be found at a number of stores adjacent to the entrance of the park, while more comprehensive supplies are found in Sorrento, 35 kilometres away.

Facilities

Because it is one of B.C.'s largest provincial parks, the facilities offered at Shuswap Lake are comprehensive and include 271 camping spots suitable for every type of recreational vehicle, flush and pit toilets, sani-station, showers, and full disabled access. The camping spots are found in a dense second-growth forest of Douglas fir, aspen, white birch, and western red cedar. Reservations are accepted and strongly advised, as BC Parks says Shuswap Lake operates at full capacity from mid-July to Labour Day (early September). This large provincial park is one of only four located on the lake that have vehicle/tent camping. The others are Herald (51 spaces), Silver Beach (35 spaces), and Yard Creek (65 spaces). If you find Shuswap full, Yard Creek is the best bet for finding space. There are also wilderness campgrounds, only accessible by boat, at six locations on the lake.

Recreational activities

Hiking

There is not really any true hiking to be had at Shuswap. Adjacent to the campground is a small nature trail, and there is a perimeter trail running near the park boundary, but neither takes more than an hour to complete. The perimeter trail had little to commend it as I found myself walking by a large metal fence for a good portion of the way. There is a 3-kilometre trail on Copper Island that takes hikers to a viewpoint of the lake and area (remember the waterproof camera). During the summer, mule deer inhabit Copper Island. There are also short trails at Roderick Haig-Brown Provincial Park (see below).

Cycling

One of the most popular recreational pursuits here is cycling, as there are over 11 kilometres of paved road in the park itself, and a mountain-bike trail has been developed.

Fishing

The entire Shuswap Lake system is known for good game-fish species including rainbow, lake, and brook trout and kokanee salmon, squawfish, burbot, carp, whitefish, and suckers. The best fishing months are May to June and October to November.

Boating

Water sports are actively undertaken here. There is a boat launch, and the waters attract powerboats, water-skiers, canoes, kayaks, windsurfers, jet-skies, and houseboats. As one would expect, the waters are particularly busy near the campground and where the arms of the lake meet at Cinnemousun Narrows, but as there are four long arms to Shuswap Lake, it does not take too long to escape the crowd. You can rent canoes or kayaks at commercial outlets adjacent to the campground. Unfortunately the dreaded jet-ski can also be rented nearby. While there is no overnight boat mooring at Shuswap Lake, nearby Shuswap Lake Provincial Marine

Park offers this facility as well as six separate developed and eight undeveloped camping locations along all four arms of the lake.

Family activities

This is the place for family fun, which centres around the kilometre-long beach. A safe swimming area with beautiful sands, warm waters, and two diving platforms is the most popular area of the park from 9:00 a.m. until well into the evening hours. Shuswap Lake has a busy visitors centre where details of the park's varied and entertaining interpretative programs and Jerry Rangers programs can be found. The centre also has historical information about the area. Shuswap boasts what must be one of the largest and most comprehensive children's play areas of any provincial park and, as mentioned above, commercial recreational activities (for example kayak rentals and go-carts) are easily accessible in the surrounding area. This park has camp hosts who are inexhaustible sources of information on local activities. Often they have visited the area regularly for many years.

Activities adjacent to the park

Boaters do not have to be told about the massive expanse of lake and shoreline that is theirs to explore. For those who do not have access to this mode of transportation, Roderick Haig-Brown Provincial Park, less than 8 kilometres from Shuswap, is an alternative, especially if you plan to visit in October. This area is home to a major run of sockeye salmon. The fish return every year, but every four years the river turns red as approximately 1.5 million fish crowd into the area. During these peak years BC Parks arranges a "Salute to the Salmon," with displays and additional staff on hand to describe the event. (The next spectacle occurs in 2002.) Even if your visit does not coincide with this event, it is worth visiting the park to learn of the salmon-spawning process and to walk the trails.

Summary

As mentioned above, this area is extremely popular during the summer months and may not be to everyone's taste at this time as it presents the more commercial side to camping in BC Parks. If you have children to entertain, Shuswap Lake, with its warm summer days and fantastic beach, comes highly recommended. When I last visited there seemed to be a number of parents looking after highly contented children who ran, cycled, played, and made new friends around the campsite with boundless energy. I am sure all these children will grow up remembering the summers of their childhood as always idyllic, and I felt quite jealous of their unadulterated enthusiasm and joie de vivre. For those who want to experience the delights of Shuswap Lake from a quieter vantage point, Herald (which caters more to the older camper), Yard Creek (with no water access), and Silver Beach Provincial Parks provide more tranquil alternatives.

7. Wasa Lake

This 144-hectare, family-oriented provincial park with four beaches is within easy reach of numerous communities and external entertainment possibilities. In this respect it is not only one of the best lakeside campgrounds, but also one of the best family campgrounds. I have to admit that its situation, at the northern end of Wasa Lake in the town from which it takes its name (christened by a Finnish settler after his native town, Vasa), is not the most picturesque, but as children are rarely concerned about anything other than sun, water, sand, and the proximity of the ice-cream store, this will not be an issue for them.

History

Originally inhabited for centuries by the Ktunaxa people, the region was explored by trappers, hunters, and explorers in the late nineteenth century when the area to the south of the park was mined initially for gold, then silver, zinc, and lead. A boom occurred and by 1897 Fort Steele, 18 kilometres south of the park (see below), was a bustling community of over 4000 people. However its fortunes rapidly diminished when the railway bypassed the town and went to Cranbrook. By 1902 Fort Steele's population had fallen to 550, and it later became all but a ghost town.

Location

The park is the largest in the region and houses the administrative headquarters of BC Parks' East Kootenay District. The campground sits on Wasa Lake, a glacier-formed shallow kettle lake reputed to be one of the warmest in the province (Osoyoos Lake and Christina Lake also claim this distinction). The park has views of the Rocky Mountains to the east

Greeting you at the park entrance.

and the Purcells to the west and is 40 kilometres north of Cranbrook on Highway 93/95. In the adjacent community of Wasa there is a gas station, a store, a neighbourhood pub, and a pink ice-cream parlour—what more do you need?

Facilities

There is just one campground here, on the eastern side of the lake in an area lightly forested with ponderosa pine and Douglas fir. There are 104 large gravel camping spots, suitable for every type of vehicle. Some have the disadvantage of being near the road (which is not that busy during the evening—this is not the main highway). There is a sani-station at the northern end of the lake and flush toilets in the campground and day-use area (no showers). The park is wheelchair accessible, reservations are accepted, and from June until early September a volunteer host answers any questions campers have. During periods of heavy demand, overflow camping is permitted in the day-use area at Campers Beach, across the road from the campground.

Recreational activities

Hiking

There is basically one nature trail to be enjoyed here. The Forest of the Rainshadow is a 2.7-kilometre, self-guided, interpretative trail that takes explorers through a forest of Douglas fir and across open grasslands to good views of Wasa Lake. A recently constructed paved route, the Wasa Lions Way, provides an easy stroll through the park and surrounding community and is also great for rollerblading and cycling. This trail is popular with both campers and locals. A BC Parks staff member told me that since it was constructed, two grannies in the community of Wasa have been given rollerblades by their grandchildren so they too could enjoy it. Watch out for speeding, grey-haired, bladed women!

Cycling

Experienced, fit riders can tackle a 33-kilometre mountain-bike route with an elevation gain of 300 metres. It leads up Wolf Creek Road, then along Lazy Lake Road from Wasa Lake to Lazy Lake. Obtain details from the campground host. The ride is not recommended for children. One of the benefits of this route is the cool, refreshing waters of Lazy Lake provide a relieving swim for tired cyclists.

Fishing

The fishing here is not great. Various guidebooks and park information leaflets describe it as "poor" and "so so." Those with patience can fish for largemouth bass.

Beaches and picnic tables—a perfect vacation spot.

Boating

There is a boat launch at Campers Beach day-use area across the road from the campground.

Wildlife viewing

Wasa Slough Wildlife Sanctuary, 7 kilometres south of the provincial park, is home to waterfowl, osprey, herons, turkey vultures, and (of course) Canada geese.

Family activities

The biggest attractions here are the four marvellous, white, sandy beaches that lie within the park boundaries. Directly opposite the campground is Campers Beach, which has the additional attraction of a playground. Three more beaches, all with designated swimming areas, picnic tables, and change houses, are found on the eastern and northern shores of the lake. As they are a little farther from the accommodation, they tend to be less crowded. The amphitheatre at the campground is home to a number of interpretative programs during the summer months, and Wasa also promotes its own unique summer events such as Wasa Fun Day (fourth Saturday in May), the Rocky Mountain Triathlon (second Sunday in June), and a sand-sculpture contest (August long weekend).

Activities adjacent to the park

As previously stated, one of the advantages of Wasa is the access it grants to numerous other pastimes. Mountain biking, golf, and horseback riding are all within easy reach. One of the best excursions must be to the heritage town of Fort Steele, 18 kilometres south of the park. This turn-of-the-century settlement was almost a ghost town until the 1960s, when the provincial government recognized its potential as a heritage site. Today almost 60 buildings have been restored, including a North West Mounted Police camp, huge waterwheel, printing office, bakery, theatre, hotel, courthouse, dentist office, and other stores and houses. Stagecoach and train rides are offered. I spent five hours exploring this fascinating example of B.C. history and could have easily spent many more. Fort Steele, with its guides dressed in costumes of the day, is much like Barkerville (see Chapter 1) but had the added attraction for me of ongoing development. Some of the buildings still in their ruined state are due to be renovated in the near future. A must see.

Twenty-four kilometres southeast of Fort Steele is the Kootenay Lake Trout Hatchery where 40 percent of the rainbow trout needed to stock B.C.'s lakes are reared.

Those seeking a little piece of Europe should head to Kimberley, which has adopted a Bavarian motif, including the largest cuckoo clock in the world, on display in the town square. It plays yodelling music. With accordion music coming out of every restaurant, and enough apple strudel and veal schnitzel to feed an army, you may find this town a little over-enthusiastic, but it is tremendous fun. I spent an evening sitting outside one of the restaurants just down the road from the yodelling cuckoo clock, which goes off on the hour or whenever a passing tourist decides to feed it 25 cents. Unfortunately I'd chosen the night when coachloads of Japanese tourists decided to patronize this spectacle. Consequently I was grateful when 9:00 p.m. struck and the yodelling came to an end. Those who want to experience Bavarian culture at its height (or want to know when to avoid it) should be aware that accordion championships are staged in Kimberley during the second week in July.

Summary

BC Parks warns of three hazards at Wasa: the lake may be subject to high winds; the temperatures in the summer soar up into the 80s, so sunscreen is a must; and in the past the park has been prone to plagues of mosquitoes. The favourite food of these pests was campers. The mosquitoes arrived when the peak tourist season started (second week in July) and stayed until the majority left (end of August). A few years ago the community of Wasa started to set aside a proportion of its taxes to helicopter-spray these insects. The result was a great improvement in the quality of life for residents and campers but not for the mosquitoes. While the area still has mosquitoes, these can easily be kept at bay with repellent and are not an issue before June or in September.

8. Okanagan Lake

I have to admit that Okanagan Lake is not my own personal preference, but data from BC Parks confirm it is the most popular provincial park in the Okanagan, with 20,476 camping parties in 1997—so what do I know? My biggest problem stems from the fact that it is located relatively near a busy road, so the noise of traffic is easily audible in some sections of the campground. Having said that, it does provide easy access to a central part of the Okanagan and has wonderful vegetation, superb facilities, and a 1000-metre beach that does not have the noise problem, so perhaps I am just too picky. This is a campground that does not have an "away from it all" feel, and in this respect it is similar to Haynes Point, just down the road, or Cultus Lake in the Lower Mainland. It is a people campground, a friendly campground, and definitely a family campground.

History

The park was established in 1955 and is unique in its development. In the 1950s over 100,000 trees were planted on the barren, rocky hillside. Many of them were non-native ornamental trees such as Manitoba, silver, and Norway maples; Russian olive; Chinese elm; Lombardy poplar; and red, blue, and mountain ash. This eclectic collection, together with the natural stands of ponderosa pine and Douglas fir, provides a home to a rich variety of bird life (see below). Each year the park's popularity grows, as indeed does that of the Okanagan region.

Location

Okanagan Lake is situated in the Okanagan Basin, 24 kilometres north of Penticton between the wonderfully named communities of Peachland and Summerland. The campground is positioned on 81 hectares of hillside between the highway and the lake.

Facilities

Okanagan Lake has two campgrounds, both equipped with showers and pit and flushing toilets. There are 168 vehicle/tent spaces, 88 of them in the southern part of the campground (which is where the boat launch is located). Spaces in the southern campground range in desirability. Some have good views of the lake but are quite close together; others have the benefit of privacy provided by vegetation but are farther away from the lake. Those in the northern campground tend to be larger and more private. Situated on a hillside, higher sites are close to the road and experience traffic noise (but compensate by having excellent views), while others lower down the slope are quieter. The park is wheelchair accessible, and reservations are taken and strongly advised.

A typical campsite under the trees at Okanagan Lake Campground.

Recreational activities

Hiking

A few small trails wind through the park between the campgrounds. A pleasant (one-hour return) stroll can be taken along a lakefront, sandy trail strewn with pine cones. Sections of the sandstone cliffs along this track have unfortunately been scarred by graffiti, but despite this eyesore the route is flat, pretty, and quiet. When you take this walk you can decide what is the best bit of the beach on which to spend the rest of the day.

Fishing

There is good fishing for carp, burbot, kokanee, Rocky Mountain whitefish, and large rainbow trout.

Boating

A boat launch is situated at the southern campground, and all types of powerboats are permitted on the waters.

Wildlife viewing

The diverse collection of trees attracts a variety of bird life including hummingbirds, cedar waxwings, quail, red-shafted flickers, western meadowlarks, and Lewis woodpeckers. Gopher snakes and rattlesnakes are also found in the area.

Family activities

With over 1000 metres of lakeside beach (the better sections found nearer the northern campground) and access to what are supposed to be the warmest waters in the country, it is not surprising this location is so popular for swimming, windsurfing, sailing, picnicking, and sunbathing. Additional recreational options include a volleyball net, swings, and a vast array of interpretative programs for all the family, including "Winnie the Pooh's wild cousins" (information about bears); "Eye of newt, toe of frog" (the world of amphibians); "We're not slimy" (snakes and reptiles); "Silent wings" (owls); "Secrets under the shell" (details about painted turtles); and much more.

Activities adjacent to the park

Those who have access to a boat can travel across the waters to Okanagan Mountain Provincial Park, which has trails and marine campgrounds on over 100,000 hectares of land. Three other parks—Kickininee, Soorimpt (which has a boat launch), and Pyramid—all without camping facilities and located 8 to 10 kilometres north of Penticton, also give access to the waters of Okanagan Lake and make good alternative picnic and swimming spots. The towns of Penticton to the south and Kelowna to the north offer many commercial activities. Closer to hand is Peachland, with a beach that stretches for 7 kilometres and access to Okanagan Mountain Park where there are trails for hiking, mountain biking, or horseback riding. The town's museum is in an unusual eight-sided, turn-of-the-century Baptist church.

Summary

Okanagan Lake is an ideal camping spot for campers with children who are looking for a safe lakeside beach, or for those who want to have a central base from which to explore the Okanagan. It is the most popular campground in the region, offering all amenities in a pleasant environment. It is also very busy and in this respect is not everyone's preference. During the summer months the temperatures in this region soar into the high 80s, remaining there for weeks. The climate is extremely hot and dry, so if you are considering travelling to this region, my advice would be to avoid the busiest and hottest months (July and August) if at all possible and choose to vacation in May or September, when the weather is still good and the temperatures bearable. These are, for me, the best times to visit this popular area of B.C., especially as the trees are in blossom from mid-April until the end of May, and most of the fruit (apricots, cherries, peaches, prunes, pears, apples, and grapes) is available after mid-June.

9. Haynes Point

It is a great shame this campground in the heart of the Okanagan Basin is not larger, as it is an extremely popular location during the summer months, with the climate ensuring a pleasant stay for those who alternatively choose to visit in the spring and fall. I have to confess this is not my personal preference because of its almost urban setting. However, it is ideal for those who like the luxury of camping on a beach near a major centre of population. The town of Osoyoos is within walking distance (although the 2-kilometre walk is not a good one). This advantage, together with the proximity of some of the Okanagan's finest vineyards and fruit farms, means that from June to November fresh fruit and vegetable stands are seen at the side of the highways, ensuring succulent produce is readily available for the camper's open fire. The season starts in May when fresh asparagus, which can be found growing wild in the park, is sold by the roadside.

History

The small, 13-hectare park was created in 1962 and is named after Judge John Carmichael Haynes, who came to Osoyoos (originally known as Sooyoos) in the nineteenth century and became a renowned legal authority and land owner. He brought law and order to the gold fields of Whitehorse Creek, near Cranbrook, before moving to the Okanagan in 1860 during the Rock Creek gold rush to assist the gold commissioner and customs collector. He was subsequently appointed to the Legislative Council of B.C. and became a county court judge. Haynes built a large house in Osoyoos and established a ranch to serve the demands of the Cariboo gold miners. He lived there until his death in 1888. Prior to his lifetime, Native people lived, hunted, and fished in the area; two archaeological sites in the park provide testimony of this history. North of the park is a

Overlooking Osoyoos Lake and the campground on the spit.

sandspit over which Highway 3 runs. This route has been used for centuries by fur traders, explorers, and miners and forms part of the famous Hudson's Bay Fur Brigade Trail. Today orchards and vineyards dominate the area, with tourism contributing a major part of the economy. Veterans who settled in Oliver after the First World War established the first orchards.

Location

This very popular campground is found at the southern end of the Okanagan River Valley, in the rainshadow of the Cascade Mountains on Osoyoos Lake, just 2 kilometres from the United States border and 2 kilometres from Osoyoos on Highway 97. The park encompasses a narrow sandspit, formed by wave action, which juts out three quarters of the way into Osoyoos Lake, together with a nearby marsh. Haynes Point is signposted from Osoyoos, although the signage near the park is not great, so be careful you don't miss the turn. All services are available in Osoyoos.

Facilities

It is little wonder this is a popular retreat, as all the 41 gravel camping spots are located on the sandspit, with over half having direct access to the beach only a few metres away. While there is not extensive vegetation, the spots are widely spaced. There are both flush and pit toilets, but no sani-station or showers. The park is accessible by wheelchair. Reservations are accepted and advisable as this is a popular location with both locals and tourists. One person I met here informed me that the locals have names for all the different campsites, adding a homey feel to the campground. There is a resident campground host.

The shoreline is dotted with marsh grasses.

Recreational activities

Hiking

A small trail leads through the marsh area of the park. When I visited in 1998 it was being developed to grant greater access to the wildlife-rich area. When the water is clear, you get excellent views of the lake's fish population from the trail.

Fishing

The lake is reputed to be the warmest in the country, making it a haven for up to twenty different types of fish. Rainbow trout, whitefish, and largemouth bass are abundant. Some of these huge specimens can easily be seen from a wooden bridge that runs over the marsh area.

Boating

Access to the warm waters of Okanagan Lake must be one of the primary reasons people decide to come here; for boating enthusiasts the lake is perfect. The campground has a boat launch, and all types of powerboats and recreational craft are permitted on the lake, which regularly gets busy with windsurfers, paddlers, and powerboat operators. Expect noise from the jet-ski set as well.

Wildlife viewing

Those interested in wildlife may be rewarded by seeing the calliope hummingbird, Canada's smallest bird, as well as orioles, eastern kingbirds, and Californian quail. In the marsh area of the park, visitors may see canyon wrens and white-throated swifts. Other unusual creatures found in the

A small wooden bridge runs over the marsh area so you can spy on the fish.

area include the spadefoot toad, painted turtles, rattlesnakes, and the burrowing owl. Information boards at the park entrance give details about the appearance and habits of these animals.

Family activities
While adults enjoy this facility during the shoulder seasons, at other times it is primarily geared to those who have young children. Easy access to the safe waters of the lake, coupled with the excellent climate of the region, means many happy families need look no farther than the sun, sea, and sand provided at Haynes Point. For those who just visit for the day, a change house is available in the day-use area. During the summer, visitors programs offer details of the unique dry environment of the region and of the unusual bird and animal life that can be found here.

Activities adjacent to the park
As mentioned above, the Spanish-themed town of Osoyoos, with many stucco buildings and red-tiled roofs, is only 2 kilometres away. A small museum is one of the town's few tourist attractions. Originally an 1891 log schoolhouse, it has a mixture of displays on topics including the history of irrigation, the history of B.C.'s provincial police, bird specimens, and Native artefacts. Osoyoos is the fruit capital of Canada. The season starts in June with cherries, followed by apricots, peaches, plums, apples, and grapes. The area also has Canada's only banana farm and must contain the highest number of fruit stands anywhere in the country. The warm climate and lack of precipitation promote desert-loving plants such as ponderosa pine, bear cacti, sagegrass, and greasewood. Just south of Oliver is a Federal Ecological Reserve—a "pocket desert." It may be difficult to find, as when I visited there were no signposts, but once I discovered it I found the area fascinating. It supports subtropical flora and fauna such as cacti, horned lizards, rattlesnakes, and burrowing owls.

A further activity of the area is wine tasting, as there are a large number of vineyards in the vicinity. The Osoyoos tourist office has numerous leaflets and magazines about wine tours in the area.

Summary
If you want to be sure of sun, sea, sand, and people during your summer vacation, make sure you book Haynes Point well in advance, as this campground is frequently full. It is a place for families, for boaters, or for people who just want to sit by a lakeside and watch others for the day. Haynes Point is not a place to visit if you want seclusion or quiet. One of the biggest disadvantages is that traffic noise or music from the nearby town can be easily heard. If you plan to stay in the summer months, be warned the temperatures can be in the high 80s for weeks, so pack the sunscreen.

10. Kokanee Creek

It is difficult to find a negative comment about Kokanee Creek Provincial Park. Some campgrounds are in fantastic locations but away from major centres of activity, so campers must bring their own entertainment; others have little to offer in their own environment but are conveniently situated for exploration of the surrounding area. Kokanee Creek provides hundreds of activities both within its boundaries and in its immediate area. And its huge, white, sandy beach makes it one of the best lakeside campgrounds in the province. It is easy to spend two weeks here and not run out of things to do even if it rains.

Kokanee Creek is the centre of the kokanee salmon spawning activity, which takes place in late August and September. When I stayed one September it was not just the bright red salmon that were putting on a show. Their performance in the water was surpassed by a couple of ospreys who circled overhead, then dived into the waters of the creek only a few feet away from our vantage point, precariously flying away with huge salmon in their beaks. While it is sad that a few of these fish, who have travelled so far with the sole thought of spawning, will meet their demise so close to their destination, the spectacle was straight from a *National Geographic* television program. The area is noted for having one of the highest osprey populations in North America.

History

The word *kokanee* means "red fish" in the Ktunaxa language and is the name given to the freshwater salmon that spawn in large numbers in the area. First Nations people inhabited the area many years ago and harvested these fish for the winter. At the turn of the century the region became popular with newcomers as gold and silver deposits were found in the surrounding hills and creeks. Legends tell of prospectors with names such as "Dirty Face Johnson" and "Dutch Charlie" who explored the area in search of precious metals. This exploration led to the development of some sizeable towns, such as Nelson. The park was created in 1955.

Location

Kokanee Creek is in the Kootenay area of the province—an area often overlooked by tourists who prefer to vacation in the Rockies or on the coast. This means the region is generally quieter than others, a real advantage if you choose to travel in the summer months. The provincial park is situated among the beautiful scenery of the Slocan Range of the Selkirk Mountains, on the western arm of massive Kootenay Lake, 19 kilometres north of Nelson on Highway 3. Services are conveniently located in Nelson or Balfour (12 kilometres to the south).

This bridge above Kokanee Creek
shows the tumbling waters below.
The bridge can be seen in the photo
of the creek to the right.

Facilities

Kokanee Creek provides 132 wooded camping spots in two locations: Sandspit (numbers 1 to 113) and Redfish (114 to 132). Redfish is closer to the road, making Sandspit my personal preference. Sandspit may also be preferable for campers with kids as it is nearer the beach and playground, with a few sites overlooking the playground, and it does not entail crossing a main road to get to the beach. Kokanee Creek is home to the West Kootenay Visitors Centre, so the facilities here are good and include flush toilets, a sani-station, and disabled access. There are no showers. Reservations are accepted. The camping spots themselves are large enough to accommodate every type of recreational vehicle, and group camping is also available.

Recreational activities

Hiking

There are a number of small (20 to 60 minute) trails that zigzag around the park, taking explorers to views of the spawning channels and to the beach. For those who demand a more serious stretch of the legs, Kokanee

Glacier Provincial Park is a 32,000-hectare area with an extensive trail system. A leaflet describing these hikes is available from the visitors centre.

Fishing

The fishing here is reputed to be second to none for both rainbow trout and kokanee, and the locals claim that the world's largest rainbow trout (4.5 kilograms/10 pounds) was landed here. Dolly Varden, char, burbot, and whitefish are also regularly taken from the lake and nearby waterways.

Boating

The campground is equipped with a boat launch, and the lake is popular with kayakers, jet-skiers, canoeists, powerboaters, water-skiers, and windsurfers. Fortunately its huge area means it never gets crowded (although the noise of the jet-skiers can be irritating if you are planning a quiet time on the beach).

Family activities

This provincial park is a delight for anyone with children, who will not want to return home from this paradise. There are a number of beautiful, long, sandy beaches, picnic facilities, changing rooms, a safe swimming area, and a children's play area. The visitors centre has displays on salmon spawning, and when I visited one June it had a live bear trap on display outside. BC Parks staff conduct walks, presentations, and talks about the area and are often on the trails as well to answer any immediate questions visitors have. Interpretative programs are offered throughout the summer.

*This bear trap is a reminder that we share the park with the bears.
Always be cautious when you are enjoying the outdoors.*

Activities adjacent to the park

One of the joys of staying here is the choice. There are hundreds of things to do and see close at hand, activities suitable for every taste and every age group. The community of Nelson is one of the oldest and certainly one of the prettiest in B.C., with the highest concentration of heritage buildings in the province. In Nelson you can visit the museum, take a self-guided walking tour, or do a pub crawl of the thirteen ale houses, all within walking distance of each other.

Kaslo, 50 kilometres to the north, is a small community with a nine-hole golf course, coffee shops and cafes, and the SS *Moyie*, the last sternwheeler on Kootenay Lake, which is now a museum. For those interested in ghost towns and early prospecting history, Sandon, along Highway 31A, is a delight to visit. It is slowly being renovated by a number of dedicated volunteers. When I visited, a gangly fourteen-year-old youth enthusiastically showed us the hydroelectric power room, complete with huge generators bought across from Manchester, England, and there was also a teashop for refreshments. Highly recommended.

Ainsworth Hot Springs, 29 kilometres north of the park, boast warm, therapeutic mineral pools and a system of caves stretching into the rock face to explore. The hot springs were completely renovated in 1998 and make a great place to visit even if the weather is bad. Cody Caves Provincial Park (no camping facilities) is located in the Selkirk Mountains above Ainsworth Hot Springs, just 11 kilometres along a good forest road off Highway 31. Visitors to the park can view spectacular cave formations including stalagmites, stalactites, waterfalls, draperies, rimstone dams, and soda straws. You are provided with the necessary protective clothing and hard hats when you take the highly informative tours offered by BC Parks.

The longest free ferry ride in the world, across Kootenay Lake from Balfour to Kootenay Bay, is just a twenty-minute drive north from the campground. If you have the opportunity, take a morning ferry and have breakfast—the trip is entertaining and the price is unbeatable.

Summary

If you are searching for a campground where you can pitch tent for a week or more, which offers swimming, sunbathing and water sports in addition to numerous other activities within an hour's drive, then look no farther than Kokanee Creek. It is an idyllic family lakeside location. One of the times I enjoy most is dusk, when the day-trippers are gone and there are quiet trails to walk on while I watch the sun go down and the stars come out. For those of us who live in the Lower Mainland, the nine-hour drive to the Kootenays may be off-putting, but it is well worth it. In addition to the camping, I regard the town of Nelson as the most beautiful in the province.

11. Crooked River

Although this provincial park falls under my choice of best lakeside campgrounds because of the 460 metres of white sandy shoreline on Bear Lake, it could easily be classed as one of the best fishing campgrounds. All through the year it attracts anglers eager to access the four lakes within its boundaries. I have stayed here twice. Once in early June, when the mosquitoes were the size of birds and my love for camping was nearly completely laid to rest as I literally sat over the smoke of our fire in a vain attempt to keep the pests at bay. The next time I stayed was in late August, when there was no sign of the insects and I could fully appreciate the beauty of Crooked River, making me question whether my previous memories were a dream. (BC Parks states that bugs can be a problem in the entire region, especially in June and July.) If you are planning a holiday here, my advice would be to remember the bug repellent or consider camping after July, when the mosquitoes have eaten their fill and moved on.

History

Crooked River Provincial Park lies in a region through which explorers Alexander Mackenzie and Simon Fraser travelled. The provincial park was established in 1965 to protect an area of pristine lakes, glacial topography, and attractive landscapes. It lies on sand and gravel soil deposited by glaciers thousands of years ago. The lakes in the park were formed by the melting of massive ice blocks.

Location

Set in a gentle, undulating countryside of lodgepole pine, alder, spruce, aspen, and birch astride the Hart Highway (Highway 97), the 1016-hectare park is 70 kilometres from Prince George within the Fraser Basin. The community of Bear Lake, 2.5 kilometres from the park, has basic services including food, gas, and accommodation. Try the wholesome, good-value breakfast at the Grizzly Inn.

Facilities

Lovely camping spaces are on offer here, and no campers will

The perfect ending to a perfect day.

be disappointed with their spot. There are 90 totally private campsites suitable for every size of camping party, set amongst a forest of lodgepole pine. A few lucky ones have views of the lake. The tarmac approach road gives way to a good gravel road when you enter the camping area. During the peak holiday months, campers register with an attendant prior to entering the campground itself. There are flush and pit toilets (no showers), a sani-station, and wheelchair accessibility and the park accepts reservations.

Recreational activities

Hiking

Nine kilometres of easy, marked trail ribbon their way through the park. These trails are not long or arduous and are perfect for families. There are four main trails, each requiring approximately an hour to complete. Squaw Lake Trail takes campers to Squaw Lake, a kettle lake formed thousands of years ago as the glaciers receded and left behind huge chunks of ice that created circular lakes when they melted. From this trail it is possible to spot beaver (especially if you visit the lake first thing in the morning) muskrat, squirrels, and chipmunks. A second route leads down the willow-sided Crooked River, a route taken by Simon Fraser over a century ago. From this path a viewpoint gives you a sight of Teapot Mountain. The third and most popular trail leads around Bear Lake and is

Eskers Provincial Park is easy to reach from Crooked River.

very busy during the early evening hours, when campers take their constitutional before dark. The final trail leads to Hart Lake.

Fishing

The four lakes in the park—Bear, Skeleton, Hart, and Squaw—offer fantastic fishing for Dolly Varden, rainbow and brook trout, grayling, and Rocky Mountain whitefish. Crooked River also has good angling potential. In the winter the park is a popular spot for ice fishing.

Boating

Powerboats are not permitted on the lake, and there is no boat launch, making this a delightful place to explore the waters. When I was here, visitors could rent bright yellow paddle boats at the day-use area ($9 per hour for a four-seater; $7 per hour for a two-seater). This is a great experience for all the family.

Wildlife viewing

Many birds visit the park including ospreys and bald eagles, and trumpeter swans in the winter. Lynx, red foxes, coyotes, and black bears also call the region home but are rarely seen near the campground.

Family activities

Bear Lake is ringed by a white sand beach created thousands of years ago by glaciers that carried fine particles of rocks and boulders. When the ice melted, the sand was deposited and now forms over 400 metres of lovely safe beach. Happily, the absence of powerboats makes it quiet, although the noise of traffic and trains is audible. Swimming, sandcastle construction, sunbathing, and burying Dad in the sand are the main activities here. A smaller beach adjacent to the campground has a change house, numerous picnic tables, an adventure playground, and a horseshoe pit close at hand. The larger beach is across the lake in the day-use area. If the weather is good you cannot find a better location for lakeshore camping.

Activities adjacent to the park

Although there are no notable communities to explore close by, there are a number of other interesting provincial parks in the region. About 50 kilometres north of Crooked River is Whiskers Point Provincial Park, which allows powerboats on the lake. This campground has 69 spaces and a beach but is subject to windier conditions than Crooked River. This is something to bear in mind if the mosquitoes are bad at Crooked River, as the wind keeps the bugs away. The facilities at Whiskers Point are similar to those at Crooked River.

Travellers who love wildlife should take a trip to Eskers Provincial Park, 40 kilometres north of Prince George (approximately 90 minutes south of Crooked River), which is a wonderful wildlife sanctuary. The park's diverse forest and natural lakes provide an environment for moose, deer, black bear, grouse, and loads of waterfowl. A 10-kilometre, wheelchair-accessible trail leads to many viewing platforms and interpretative boards. Eskers is an informative provincial park (no camping), well worth a visit in any season.

Summary

Crooked River is not the largest lakeside campground but is certainly one of the quietest. It is a great safe place for young families to come and make new friends for two days or two weeks. While it may not be that appealing for those who seek organized activities, who yearn to be near large centres of population, or who wish to annoy the world by bombing around on their jet-skis, it is inviting for the rest of us who do not require these activities to have a good time. During late September the colours here are wonderful; although the lake may be a bit cool for swimming at this time, the tranquillity and scenery will compensate.

Additional Recommendations

The Best Family Campgrounds All the campgrounds described in Chapter 1, with the exception of Barkerville, are located at lakesides.

Lakelse See Chapter 4.

Fintry and Blanket Creek See Chapter 5.

Paarens Beach/Sowchea See Chapter 6.

Mabel Lake (Okanagan). Situated in a cooler region of the Okanagan, this campground has 81 spaces adjacent to 2000 metres of shoreline, including a beach.

Moyie Lake (Rockies). Although it boasts a popular beach, the lake is somewhat crowded with powerboats. The campground has 104 spaces and all amenities.

Purden Lake (North by Northwest) For families in Prince George, this is a conveniently located, 78-space campground with fantastic swimming and lake-related activities.

Beaumont (North by Northwest) First-rate swimming and fishing can be had at this 49-site location 130 kilometres east of Prince George.

THE BEST HIKING CAMPGROUNDS

The one thing these four campgrounds have in common is their vast area, with developed trails and wilderness campgrounds that grant the dedicated backpacker access to some of the most remote areas of the province. The information in the following pages does not do justice to the numerous walks and hikes that can be undertaken in these parks. Instead I decided to give examples of the types of hikes on offer, from fifteen-minute strolls to five-day or longer wilderness excursions. BC Parks produces information leaflets on all four parks, with maps, trail lengths, and other pertinent information. You can obtain further details by talking to the BC Parks representatives at each of the campgrounds about trail conditions, weather, and difficulty.

Mount Robson, the "Monarch of the Canadian Rockies," is a massive provincial park and probably the most popular of the four in this section, with over 170 developed camping spots and some wonderful trails. Wells Gray, known as the Waterfall Park, has both hiking and canoeing possibilities. It is less well known than Robson but just as spectacular. Yoho National Park in the Rockies provides not only hiking trails but also a number of camping locations and a rich history of railroad development. Finally Tweedsmuir, the largest provincial park in B.C., has few developed camping spots (42), but like all the others offers numerous rustic camping locations and some true wilderness scenery hundreds of miles from any large population centres.

12. Mount Robson

I can vividly recall my first visit to Mount Robson Provincial Park and the audible gasp my companion and I simultaneously emitted as we took the turn on the Yellowhead Highway heading east and Mount Robson came into view. Our awe was similar to that expressed by many others, including the British explorer W.B. Cheadle, who recorded one of the first accounts of the peak: "We saw its upper portion dimmed by a necklace of light, feathery clouds, beyond which its painted apex of ice, glittering in the morning sun, shot up into the blue heaven above." Mount Robson is, in my opinion, one of the most beautiful sights in B.C. The highest peak in the Rockies at almost 4000 metres, it deserves its title, Monarch of the Canadian Rockies. If you are thinking of visiting, my advice is don't think twice—just go. Like other large provincial parks such as Strathcona on Vancouver Island and Manning in southwestern B.C., Robson not only provides excellent camping facilities and easy access to the B.C. wilderness, but also has conveniently situated commercial facilities that give campers the option of eating away from the campfire as well as the comfort of knowing that forgotten groceries or camping supplies are near at hand. No matter how many times I visit, I never tire of this place.

History

The local First Nations people christened Robson *Yuh-hai-has-hun*, the Mountain of the Spiral Road. There is debate over whether the more recent name owes its origins to Colin Robertson, a Hudson's Bay factor and member of parliament who dispatched the Iroquois to look for fur in the area in 1820, or John Robson, premier of B.C. from 1889 to 1892. In 1913 the B.C. legislature passed a special act to ensure this area of exceptional beauty would be preserved for all to enjoy. Later that year the first trail, from Robson River to Berg Lake, was constructed. It remains popular today (see below). The logging industry introduced more people into the area following the Second World War, when the communities of Valemount and McBride expanded. Today the park is popular as a stopping-off point for coachloads of tourists as they travel between Prince George and Jasper. It is also a centre for outdoor wilderness activities including mountaineering, skiing, hunting, fishing, camping, and even heli-skiing.

Location

This 219,535-hectare park, the largest provincial park in the Rockies, contains the birthplace of the mighty Fraser River, Canada's third largest river, which travels 1370 kilometres and flows into the Pacific at Vancouver. Located on the Yellowhead Highway (Highway 16), it is 290 kilometres from Prince George to the west, 390 kilometres from Edmonton to the east, and 400 kilometres from Kamloops to the south. The nearest towns

Blue skies, tall mountains, and glacier-fed rivers can all be enjoyed at Mount Robson Provincial Park.

of any size are Jasper and Valemount. While it is possible to get to Mount Robson from the Lower Mainland in a day, it is a ten-hour drive. Greyhound buses run daily through the park.

Facilities

There are three campgrounds in the park. Robson Meadow (125 spots) and Robson River (19 spots) are located at the western end of the park, have flush toilets and showers, and are wheelchair accessible. The third campground, Lucern (32 spots), is 10 kilometres west of the Alberta border. Robson River is my favourite because it is smaller than Robson Meadow but still has all amenities and is adjacent to services The sani-station is located at Robson Meadow. Most sites are large, private, and well situated in the evergreen forest. In addition to the formal campgrounds, there are primitive wilderness campgrounds in seven locations along the Berg Lake Trail. Anyone planning to use the latter facilities must pay campground fees at the visitors centre. There is a shop, gas station, and café in the park but no non-camping accommodation. For that, and for all other supplies, visit the communities of Tete Jaune Cache, Valemount, and McBride. You can reserve camping spots only at Robson Meadow and along the Berg Lake Trail.

Recreational activities

Hiking

The 44-kilometre Berg Lake Trail runs alongside the Robson River and, with its elevation gain of 795 metres to Berg Lake, is reported to be one of the most heavily used backpacking routes in the Rockies. It takes seven to ten hours to complete, although many hike as far as they can while allowing time to make it back to base by evening. As mentioned above, you must obtain a camping permit if you plan to stay at any of the campgrounds on the trail. Even those who choose to hike just the 8-kilometre return journey to Kinney Lake will be rewarded with the sight of mountain reflections in milky-blue glacial water. Those who venture farther will pass through the Valley of the Thousand Waterfalls, visit three large waterfalls, see glaciers, and complete the journey at Berg Lake, close to the Mount Robson peak. There are a number of smaller hikes in the park, such as the Yellowhead Mountain Trail (17 kilometres return). For those who want a challenge there is the 70-kilometre Moose River Route, which requires six days to complete. Maps of the trails and information on their conditions and on the weather are all available from the visitors centre.

Climbing

The first European attempt to climb Mount Robson was in 1907, but it was not until 1913 that the peak was finally conquered. Each year, experienced rock climbers pit their wits against this and other mountains in the park. BC Parks warns that only experienced and properly equipped mountaineers should attempt the mountains, glaciers, and snowfields.

Fishing

The glacial waters feeding the rivers and lakes in Robson Park do not generally yield high fish populations, but the persistent angler may be rewarded with Dolly Varden, kokanee, or rainbow trout.

Boating

Boat launches are available at Moose Lake and Yellowhead Lake.

Family activities

The Mount Robson Visitors Centre at the Mount Robson Viewpoint provides details of the park's activities, including the many interpretative programs offered by BC Parks staff throughout the summer. It also contains displays of natural and human history, and audio-visual presentations about the area. The area is rich in wildlife including moose, grizzly bears, caribou, black bears, mule deer, and over 170 species of birds. There is an adventure playground but no swimming. Mountain bikes are not permitted on the trails and neither are horses, although you can book a trail ride through commercial facilities adjacent to the park in Valemount.

Activities adjacent to the park

As mentioned above, the local communities of Tete Jaune Cache (named, like the Yellowhead Highway, after a blond fur trader of mixed white and Iroquois blood who travelled in the area in the early nineteenth century) and Valemount have commercial facilities where adventurers can arrange to go white-water rafting, canoeing, horseback riding, and wilderness exploring. Just west of the park entrance are Rearguard Falls Provincial Park and Terry Fox Provincial Park, while in the other direction, Jasper is a pleasant place to wander around if the tourists are not out in force.

Summary

If you appreciate mountain scenery and like hiking you will love Mount Robson, but be warned that the weather, even in July and August, may not be on your side—and even if the daytime weather is warm, the nights can be very cool. As the area is under a heavy blanket of snow for much of the year, the trails are late to open. As with many of the provincial parks, the best time to visit, if you can, is in the shoulder months of June and September. September is definitely the preferred month as most of the tourists have left, the trails are quieter and snow-free, and camping spaces are easily found. This is not a provincial park recommended for a long stay if you have young children to entertain. For the rest of us, it is a jewel in the provincial parks' crown and should not be missed.

Scenery like this should not be missed.

13. Wells Gray

This huge park, the fourth largest in the province, exceeds 520,000 hectares in area and is known as the Waterfall Park owing to the countless number of waterfalls that cascade within its boundaries. Visitors can easily spend a month here and only begin to realize its unique splendour. I most recently spent four wonderful days here in July 1998 and cannot wait to return. The park contains two large river systems; five huge lakes (Murtle, Mahood, Clearwater, Azure, and Hobson); numerous small lakes, rivers, streams, and waterways; and of course waterfalls, the most well known being Helmcken Falls and Dawson Falls, stunning in both summer and winter. One of the joys of this park is the vast array of scenery it offers, from floral displays in alpine meadows, which occur in the south of the park, to the almost inaccessible rugged peaks, mountains, and glaciers in the north. Wells Gray also has extinct volcanoes, lava beds, and mineral springs. As one would imagine with all this space and variety, there are countless hikes and boating, canoeing, kayaking, and fishing opportunities to be had, making Wells Gray a magnet for outdoor enthusiasts.

History

Created in 1939, the park was named after the Honourable Arthur Wellesley Gray, Minister of Lands for B.C. from 1933 to 1941. The history of the area dates back to First Nations dwellers, notably the Shuswap (Secwepemc) and Chilcotin people, who hunted and fished in the area. There are approximately 35 archaeological sites in the park. In the 1870s, Canadian Pacific Railway surveyors came to the area in search of a rail route through the mountains to the Pacific coast. When Kicking Horse Pass, farther south, was chosen in 1881, they left the region and it received little attention until the 1930s. Mining and placer gold operations in the early 1900s were followed by limited logging activity and, in the 1920s, unsuccessful attempts at farming. After the discovery of Helmcken Falls in 1913 there were calls to create a park, and in 1939 the area was awarded this status. Since the 1930s the area has become internationally known for its hunting, fishing, and scenery. When I stayed, the dominant language in the campground was German, and much of the park's information is available in English and German.

Location

There are three entrances to Wells Gray. The main one is north of the community of Clearwater (120 kilometres north of Kamloops) off Highway 5, the Yellowhead Highway. The first 40 kilometres of this access are paved, but 10 kilometres after you enter the park the road changes to a good gravel road that carries on to Clearwater Lake and two of the largest campgrounds (see "Facilities," below). This is the most popular entrance and the easiest to access.

Clearwater Lake.

The second main camping region is at Mahood Lake, in the southeast corner of the park, and is accessed from 100 Mile House on Highway 97 (the Cariboo Highway) by driving 88 kilometres on what BC Parks describes as a secondary road. (Our car had no difficulty with it.) Mahood and nearby Canim Lake are renowned fishing hotspots, so this campground attracts a number of anglers. There are no roads through the park that connect Clearwater to Mahood.

Mahood Lake.

The third access is from Blue River, 232 kilometres northeast of Kamloops, via 24 kilometres of gravel road. A 2.5-kilometre trail then leads to Murtle Lake, where there is only wilderness camping. Canoeists and kayakers are the main users of this route as it leads to the beautiful, horseshoe-shaped lake where powerboats are prohibited.

Clearwater Lake Campground's nearest full services are at Clearwater; Mahood's nearest comprehensive services are at 100 Mile House, although gas, propane, and food can be purchased at Canim Lake, a small community about twenty minutes from the campground.

Facilities

In addition to numerous wilderness camping spots, there are four campgrounds in the park. Three campgrounds are accessed from the Clearwater approach road and include the newly opened Pyramid Mountain Campground, with 50 spaces at the edge of the park; Clearwater Lake, which has 32 spots; and Falls Creek with 41 units (the last two sites are adjacent to each other). There is a sani-station at Clearwater Lake. The fourth campground is reached from the 100 Mile House entrance (off Highway 97) and has 32 spots. Facilities are the basic ones found in BC Parks (pit toilets, wood, water, picnic tables, fire pit). Reservations are accepted at Clearwater Lake Campground. There are a variety of private lodges and motels in Clearwater, Blue River, and 100 Mile House, the most famous being Helmcken Falls Lodge, an impressive 1948 log building offering food and accommodation, which you pass before the park's main Clearwater entrance. A shady verandah at the lodge is an ideal spot for a refreshing beer or bowl of ice-cream while you watch the hummingbirds feed. These communities also have grocery and camping supply stores.

Recreational activities

Hiking

The biggest attraction for me is the hiking. It is possible to take a 45-minute walk or a seven-day hiking excursion. BC Parks cautions that while a number of trails have been constructed and are well maintained, there are other routes for which some wilderness skills are required. All hikes are detailed in brochures you can pick up from the Travel Info Centre at the junction of Highway 5 and Clearwater Valley Road. Many trails start conveniently close to the campgrounds. Some of the best hikes are in the Clearwater Valley area. One of these, a four-hour hike to the base of Helmcken Falls, is not suitable for children and is somewhat rugged in places, but the journey to the falls, more than twice as high as Niagara, is well worth the effort. During the winter, when the falls freeze, visitors snowshoe or ski in to see the spectacle. For those who prefer a more leisurely pace, the falls can also be viewed by undertaking a short walk

View over the Clearwater River from Osprey Lookout.

from the parking lot at the end of Helmcken Falls Road. Other hikes include the Battle Mountain Alpine Meadows Trail, through a blanket of summer flowers if walked in August, and numerous 1- to 2-kilometre strolls to view waterfalls, lava beds, or mineral springs. From Clearwater Lake Campground it is possible to take a pleasant day's hike along Clearwater Lake, then high into the mountains and back via Chain Meadow (which is not a meadow). Be warned: BC Parks literature states this trek is 12 kilometres. It is not; it is 17 kilometres. Since I undertook the hike on a hot July day while five months pregnant, I did not appreciate this typing error in their literature!

Fishing

As you would expect with so many waterways, rivers, and lakes, the fishing here is excellent. Rainbow trout, Dolly Varden, and lake trout inhabit most of the park's waters. BC Parks staff say the most productive locations are Canim River, Mahood Lake, Murtle Lake, and Murtle River. Therefore, as mentioned above, if you are an angler you may decide to head straight to Mahood Lake Campground. For those with a passion for fly fishing, Canim and Mahood Rivers, as well as a number of other rivers in the vicinity, have fly-casting possibilities.

Boating

Clearwater, Hobson, Azure, Mahood, and Murtle Lakes were formed centuries ago by glacial erosion. Today the combined area of these lakes is approximately 22,000 hectares. Murtle Lake lies in the Murtle Lake Nature Conservatory, where motorized transportation is prohibited, giving it a serene and tranquil air. It is considered by some to be one of the most beautiful wilderness lakes in B.C. Clearwater and Azure Lakes are each about 26 kilometres long and are joined by a small portage. Both have numerous wilderness campgrounds and small beaches. Powerboats are permitted on Mahood, Azure, and Clearwater Lakes. There are boat launches at Mahood and Clearwater Lakes. At Clearwater Lake Campground, commercial operators rent canoes and kayaks ($25 for a half day and $35 full day) and arrange four-hour powerboat excursions up Clearwater Lake to Rainbow Falls ($40). These are 1998 prices.

Family activities

Overall, Wells Gray is not geared towards those who have small children to entertain, but if your kids like paddling and hiking, they will definitely have fun here. BC Parks interpreters are on hand in July and August at Dawson Falls, Helmcken Falls, and Clearwater Lake to provide details of the fauna and flora of the area as well as the geological and human history. They also arrange guided walks and talks. There are no formal beaches accessible from the two main campgrounds, although small beaches can be found along the lakeshores. You can swim at 24-kilometre-long Mahood Lake—although the lake is situated in a steep-sided U-shaped valley between the Quesnel and Shuswap Highlands, there are several beaches to be found and a shelved foreshore for easy swimming access. Finally, commercial operators at Helmcken Lodge and 100 Mile House offer guided horseback riding excursions into the park.

Activities adjacent to the park

The communities of Clearwater (population 7000) and Blue River (population 300) have grown as centres of commercial activity for Wells Gray Provincial Park. You can arrange white-water rafting, canoe trips, trail rides, hiking expeditions, fishing, snowmobiling, and skiing excursions in these towns. Clearwater also houses the Yellowhead museum, with Native artefacts, pioneer antiques, and natural history displays. There is a golf course near Helmcken Lodge.

Summary

According to a BC Parks staffperson I spoke to when visiting Wells Gray, the park has 56 animal species (including the largest remaining population of mountain caribou in southern B.C.), over 200 species of birds, over 200 types of mushrooms, and over 700 types of plants. For those who want to escape the crowds and experience the true beauty of B.C., Wells Gray certainly delivers. Those considering spending some time may wish to read Roland Neave's book *Exploring Wells Gray Park*, published by the Friends of Wells Gray Park, which provides excellent descriptions of every aspect of the park.

14. Yoho National

Yoho National Park is a spectacular location for a camping holiday, regarded by many as comparable to the Swiss Alps. It takes its name from a Cree word that expresses awe and wonder. Along with Banff, Jasper, and Kootenay Parks, Yoho has been designated a World Heritage Site by UNESCO. The site is one of the largest protected mountainous regions in the world. Yoho is the smallest of the four contiguous parks and is Canada's second oldest national park. Situated on the western slopes of the Rockies, with its eastern boundary on the Great Divide, Yoho's 131,000 hectares contain lakes, mountains (28 with peaks reaching over 3000 metres), icefields, waterfalls, glaciers, rivers, and alpine meadows—a wealth of geological wonders to explore.

History

Yoho's development as a national park is directly related to Canada's need for a railway link from coast to coast. In the 1870s a route through the steep Kicking Horse Pass was chosen for the Canadian Pacific Railway, which was completed in 1885. The track passed through some breathtaking scenery, and when federal government officials and railway executives learned that the chosen route skirted some natural hot springs, they saw the opportunity to create Canada's first national park, Banff, in 1885. The Mount Stephen Reserve, another scenic spot along the rail route, was opened a year later, and the CPR established a hotel at Field to cater to climbers, tourists, and artists who visited the area at the turn of the century. In 1911 Mount Stephen Reserve was renamed Yoho.

Location

Yoho is located on the Trans-Canada Highway between Golden and Lake Louise. Services can be found in the community of Field, which also has comprehensive information on the park. Adjacent to the Kicking Horse Campground is a small restaurant/coffee shop that sells camping supplies. A private lodge with restaurant and coffee bar operates at Emerald Lake.

Facilities

Compared to other areas at a lower altitude, Yoho's camping season starts late and does not get into full swing until the end of June. There are five campgrounds to choose from, offering over 300 sites. The first to open (mid-May to mid-October) is Kicking Horse, 5 kilometres east of Field, which is the only one with showers (coin operated). It has pit toilets, a sani-station, relatively small campsites suitable for small vehicles and tents, and a large open "corral" area for RVs (86 spaces in total). Chancellor Peak Campground, 5 kilometres from the western park boundary, opens the last week in May until September 20 and has 58 sites, some close to

Grab a spot on the riverside at Chancellor Peak Campground.

the rushing azure-blue waters of the Kicking Horse River, with lovely mountain views. The sites are quite open, and pit toilets, water, wood, fire pits, and picnic tables are located here. The largest campground is Hoodoo Creek, with 106 densely wooded, peaceful sites, flush toilets, and sani-station. It is located 7 kilometres from the western entrance of the park and is open from the end of June until early September. Monarch Campground is adjacent to Kicking Horse, has 46 sites and pit toilets, and operates from the end of June until the beginning of September. Sites here can accommodate all sizes of vehicle, but noise from Highway 1 is audible. The final campground is Takakkaw Falls, a walk-in campground with 35 spaces, open from the last week in June until the last week in September. A number of primitive camping spaces are also available throughout the park for those exploring the back country. Park-use permits are required for overnight camping and there is a $3 charge for firewood.

Recreational activities

Hiking

Yoho is a hiker's paradise, with over 500 kilometres of trails, many considered to be the best in the Rockies. Anyone considering walking in the region should make the visitors centre in Field the first point of call. You can pick up a detailed map of the hiking trails and can register if you plan to hike or camp in the back country. If you do not want to undertake taxing multi-day hikes, there are a number of gorgeous day excursions.

Emerald Lake is a good base from which to commence these. Trails lead from the lake to Yoho and Burgess Passes, as well as to breathtaking Hamilton Lake. When I last visited I hiked the Iceline Trail (one day), which starts from Takakkaw Falls and takes you past glaciers, alpine meadows, forests, and waterfalls. Most of the elevation gain occurs in the first couple of hours, after which the views are superb. One attraction on this hike is the resident of a remote cabin who supplies drinks and fresh-baked goods to weary walkers. Located 7 kilometres from the nearest road, the baker uses horses to bring in provisions. Larch Valley is another day-long hike with a fantastic reputation. For those with less stamina, shorter recom-

Takakkaw Falls are magnificent.

mended walks include an hour-long trail around Emerald Lake (said to be one of the most beautiful lakes in the Rockies), a 2.4-kilometre hike to Wapta Falls (22 kilometres west of Field), and a ten-minute walk to Takakkaw Falls, one of Canada's highest waterfalls at 384 metres, which takes its name from the Cree word for "magnificent." There are great photographic opportunities here, and a number of the longer day hikes start from Takakkaw Falls.

Fishing

As the waters of the park are glacial and not stocked, the fishing here is not great, although it is possible to catch trout in lakes and streams away from the glaciers.

Boating

Only non-motorized craft are permitted. Canoeing is a pleasant option on both Lake O'Hara and Emerald Lake. You can rent a canoe at Emerald Lake.

Wildlife viewing

A 1998 Parks Canada Guide gave the following estimates of the animal population in Yoho: 6 to 10 grizzly bears; 15 to 25 black bears; 5 to 10 grey wolves; 25 to 50 elk; 40 to 60 moose; 300 to 400 mountain goats. Coyotes and mule deer also reside here. Early and late in the day are the best times for observation.

Grizzly bears have large humps on their shoulders.

Family activities

A broad range of interpretative programs are offered in Yoho from July 1 to September 1, including a guided walk around Emerald Lake and a 1.5-hour walk from Kicking Horse Campground that details the development of the railway. Kicking Horse and Hoodoo have evening programs, and Kicking Horse has a children's play area. Cycling, horseback riding, and white-water rafting are available from commercial outlets nearby. Check out the visitors centre for full operating times and prices.

Activities adjacent to the park

In addition to the activities available in the park, Yoho is an excellent base from which to explore other national parks including Kootenay (see Chapter 4), Glacier, and Banff. The tourist town of Lake Louise lies just outside the park boundaries.

Summary

In the summer of 1884, 12,000 men came to the Rockies, working fourteen hours a day blasting through rock, clearing, cutting, and burning to establish a rail link through the Kicking Horse Pass. As a result, Yoho is a park with intimate ties to the railroad. Viewpoints and interpretative boards within its boundaries illustrate the accomplishments of the CPR's employees, with the famous Spiral Tunnels east of Kicking Horse Campground providing testimony to the engineers' ability and ingenuity. Yoho, like Jasper and Banff in Alberta, is a hiker's dream. Those with a passion for this pursuit can trek between these three parks for days. Statistics show that 0.7 million people visit Yoho each year, though few explore the longer trails or even the day-long hikes. While Yoho may be regarded as the Switzerland of North America, an advantage it has over its European cousin is its lack of visitors—a real advantage for those of us who want to appreciate its natural splendour.

15. Tweedsmuir (South)

This is the giant of B.C. provincial parks, covering 974,046 hectares and stretching over 225 kilometres from north to south. As you can imagine with a park this size, there are loads of things to see and do, although much of it is difficult to access. It has been divided into two sections, north and south, with only the southern section easily accessible by road. The geography of this land is extremely varied. To the east are the 1350-metre peaks of the Rainbow Range of mountains. Formed from eroded lava and fragmented rock, their colour is an unbelievable mix of reds, oranges, lilacs, purples and yellows. This is one of the most well-known features of Tweedsmuir and frequently appears in photographs promoting the region. The western section of the park contains the higher and more rugged Coast Mountains, including Monarch Mountain, the highest mountain in the park at 3533 metres. Tweedsmuir is a true wilderness park, ideal for canoeing, fishing, hiking, and backpacking amongst some of the most remote, spectacular scenery in the province. This is not a park for those who seek the comforts of civilization.

History

The park is named after John Buchan, Baron Tweedsmuir of Elsfield, Canada's fifteenth Governor General, who travelled through the area in 1937. The first inhabitants were people of the Bella Coola (Nuxalk) and Chilcotin First Nations, who fished for salmon in the highly productive waters. The first non-Native to traverse the region was Alexander Mackenzie in 1793. Mackenzie and his colleagues travelled overland from the Fraser River, across the Interior Plateau, and through the Rainbow Range to reach the Pacific. They relied on the skills of local Native guides and followed aboriginal trading routes to reach their destination. Hikers with considerable stamina can retrace Mackenzie's steps today by tackling the 420-kilometre Mackenzie Heritage Trail (recommended time: 30 days), what the Native people called the Grease Trail. Those without the stamina may just decide to read about it, as Mackenzie kept a diary of his journey.

Location

Tweedsmuir is 480 kilometres by air from Vancouver and is roughly triangular in shape, bounded by the Ootsa-Whitesail Lakes to the north, the Coast Mountains to the west, and the Interior Plateau to the east. If you aren't flying, go overland on Highway 20, which runs between Williams Lake and Bella Coola. Tweedsmuir is 360 kilometres west of Williams Lake. Be prepared for a bumpy ride as the highway contains many gravel sections with numerous switchbacks.

Facilities

Despite its size, South Tweedsmuir does not offer an abundance of camping spaces; there are only two small campgrounds suitable for RVs, although a number of wilderness sites are available in the park. The first campground with facilities for all is Atnarko, which has 28 sites set amidst a grove of old-growth Douglas fir, 28 kilometres from the eastern entrance to the park. The second is Fisheries Pool, located near the small community of Stuie, 44 kilometres from the eastern entrance, with 14 spaces. Facilities include a sani-station, pit toilets, wood, fire pits, picnic tables, and pump water. The town of Bella Coola, 50 kilometres west of the park, has all services, while two private lodges offer gas, accommodation, groceries, and restaurants.

Recreational activities

Hiking

Anyone considering hiking in this area should collect the numerous leaflets produced by BC Parks that detail the options, available from the park headquarters near the Atnarko River Campground. One of the most popular day hikes is the Rainbow Range Trail, which provides easy access into an alpine environment and takes about six hours (16 kilometres return). The Rainbow Range trailhead, east of the campground, also grants access to much longer, more strenuous hikes and is one of the starting points for numerous trails (a leaflet entitled "Rainbow Range" gives maps and details of these). Another starting point is Hunlen Falls, adjacent to Atnarko Campground, which may be the campground of choice if you plan to hike this area. Many of the shorter walks start from the private lodges at Stuie. Bear in mind that the snow is slow to leave the area; the best hiking time is from mid-July until mid-September.

Fishing

Fishing is one of the most popular activities in the park, for both people and grizzly bears. Coho and chinook salmon, steelhead, and trout can be caught in the Atnarko and Bella Coola Rivers, while the Dean River is good for fly fishing. Lakes in the region contain cutthroat and rainbow trout, Dolly Varden, and whitefish. Trout fishing in Turner Lake is reputed to be excellent. For the rich and adventurous, a number of private guides offer to fly anglers to remote lakes.

Boating

There is a car-top boat launch at Fisheries Pool, and you can rent canoes at Turner Lake. From Turner Lake it is possible to canoe through a series of quiet waterways and lakes. BC Parks states all portages are short, easy, with little elevation gain. Many hiking trails also lead from Turner Lake, so it is possible to combine hiking and canoeing pursuits.

Hiking in Tweedsmuir Provincial Park.

Wildlife viewing

Moose, deer, caribou, wolves, cougars, black bears, and grizzly bears all inhabit the park. During the salmon-spawning season (September to October), grizzlies are often seen along the Dean, Bella Coola, and Atnarko Rivers.

Family activities

This park is not oriented towards children, although the two private lodges rent canoes and offer horseback excursions, which are attractive to every age group.

Activities adjacent to the park

Bella Coola lies on North Bentinck Arm, which leads to the Pacific Ocean. As the main port between Vancouver and Prince Rupert, its waterfront is an interesting collection of water-based activities, a museum, seafood restaurant, and Native craft store.

Summary

South Tweedsmuir is reputed to have some of the most breathtaking scenery in North America, but as it is more remote than the national parks of the Rockies, it does not attract the same crowds. I visited during the peak month of July, and it was not at all busy. For those who really want to experience the remote outdoors, this is the place to go. As far as I was concerned, the region's only disadvantage was the insect population, which can be quite fierce at certain times. Bug spray should definitely be on your list if you plan to travel in Tweedsmuir, but this should not prevent you from visiting.

Additional Recommendations

Naikoon See Chapter 6.

Glacier National (High Country) With 21 hiking trails crossing over 140 kilometres, this is a great place to hike and camp, but be aware: because of the altitude, the 79 camping spots in two locations are not open until mid-June.

Cathedral (Okanagan) This is a relatively small, sixteen-space campground with only wilderness camping available but with access to some beautiful hikes amongst spectacular scenery.

THE BEST HOT SPRINGS CAMPGROUNDS

I am cheating a little in this section, as the four campgrounds included here are not only the best—they are the *only* parks with hot springs outside B.C.'s Lower Mainland. I reckon they are all pretty perfect places to spend a camping vacation, with or without the advantage of hot springs, and they are extremely diverse in the provisions they offer the camper.

Liard River is not only the best hot springs campground, but I believe it is the best campground in the province, with the only disadvantage being its remote northerly location. For those who are travelling the Alaska Highway, its two pools are a refreshing break from driving. Lakelse Lake Provincial Park not only has hot springs within 3 kilometres of its gates, but it also has a beach and spacious, well-kept camping spots. Those with children would find this an ideal location. Kootenay is a massive national park, which in addition to housing probably the best-known hot springs in the province (Radium), also offers a wealth of outdoor pursuits for those who seek wilderness adventures. In contrast to the other three, Whiteswan Lake Provincial Park is the most undeveloped, a quiet, little-known place devoid of commercial interference, close to the white waters of Lussier Creek.

16. Liard River Hotsprings

I discovered Liard River Hotsprings by chance five years after I had moved to B.C., when I was sure my enthusiasm for BC Parks' facilities could rise no higher. As we drove north on Highway 37, I was reading the map in search of a campground for the evening and matched number 163 with the name Liard River Hotsprings. What I imagined was a roadside campground with a bubbling pool, two metres in diameter, for which the campground had been named. How wrong you can be! Certain memories cannot be eroded, and such is my experience with Liard River. Although I have only visited once, its beauty and magical location are stamped indelibly in my mind and I long to return to this haven. Having sung its praises, I must admit this campground will not appeal to everyone, as it has little to offer other than the hot springs. Those who seek hiking, fishing, and canoeing will be disappointed. The rest of us will be in heaven.

History

The source of the hot springs is not known for sure, but it is believed that they are the result of groundwater circulating deep under the earth's surface. The water is heated by the earth's core and then returns to the surface via cracks in the rock to form warm pools. In 1957 a provincial park was created, encompassing 668 hectares surrounding the hot springs, so that the unique habitat could be protected and enjoyed forever. While this formally recognized the value of the hot springs, travellers have known about these pools for centuries. Many hundreds of years ago the people of the Kaska Nation bathed here, while in 1835 Robert Campbell, a Hudson's Bay Company factor, made a record of the waters, and the trappers and prospectors who worked in the area made use of them. In 1942 the American Army, stationed in the area to build the Alaska Highway, constructed the first boardwalk to the pools. When I stayed here, construction workers garrisoned nearby to resurface sections of the Alaska Highway were one of the main user groups, recapturing the joy their American predecessors had experienced 50 years before.

Just a few kilometres north of the park lies the southern perimeter of B.C.'s second-largest forest fire, caused by lightning, which burned 182,725 hectares of land in 1982. Today the area is covered by low scrub and, in the summer, beautiful wild flowers.

Location

As previously stated, this beautiful park's only disadvantage is that it is the most northerly in B.C. and therefore not easily accessible to the majority of the population of the province. Anyone who does travel this far on the Alaska Highway will be amply rewarded for the effort. The second largest hot springs in Canada (after Banff), Liard River is situated at Mile 496 of

Liard River Hotsprings invites you to enjoy a little bit of heaven.

the highway, 20 kilometres north of Muncho Lake Provincial Park (see Chapter 6). A restaurant and small shop are located across the road from the park itself; more comprehensive services can be found at the town of Muncho Lake, 56 kilometres away.

Facilities

Fifty-three large, well-appointed, private campsites suitable for every type of recreational vehicle are set among trees. Although the campground is quite near the road, there is not a lot of traffic so noise, especially at night, is not an issue. There is no sani-station, and the park is wheelchair accessible. Facilities are restricted to the basic ones (fire pit, wood, water, pit toilets, picnic tables). Reservations are accepted and advisable as the park is popular with tourists travelling along the Alaska Highway. There are no showers…but who needs them!

Recreational activities

Hot springs

The biggest attraction at this park is, of course, the hot springs, which have been beautifully maintained in their natural setting. A delightful boardwalk takes campers from the campground, across warm-water swamps, to two bathing pools, both with change rooms. At the larger Alpha pool, bathers can choose which area of the water to sit in and which temperature to endure, from an almost unbearable 53 degrees where the waters emerge, to a more comfortable heat farther from the inflow. Submerged wooden benches have been positioned at various points through the pools, and there is a lovely waterfall to sit up against. The smaller Beta circular pool, a twelve-minute walk from the campground, is a constant temperature (approximately 42 degrees). It is possible to swim here, or you can sit on submerged wooden steps that lead into the pool. The smell of sulphur is more concentrated at the Beta pool, which does not get as crowded as the other. Soaps and shampoos are prohibited, as is alcohol.

One of the delights of relaxing in these therapeutic mineral waters is the conversation that you can strike up with fellow travellers and locals. One Native Canadian who lived in the area informed me he regularly visited the pools just for the interesting conversation. He also told me of other undeveloped hot springs in the surrounding mountains. There is something about relaxing, semi-naked, under the stars in warm waters that induces dialogue with fellow human beings.

Plant and wildlife viewing

In addition to these two mineral pools, a variety of fauna and flora unique to the area can be seen. Over 250 species of boreal forest plants grow here, including 14 species of orchids. At certain times of the year a hanging garden near Alpha pool is a showcase of this vegetation, loved by photographers. The garden can be accessed from the boardwalk, and interpretative boards within the park provide details about the flowers and the unique geological forms on which they have grown.

More than 100 bird species visit the park, while moose and black bear also inhabit the area. In 1997 Liard River was the scene of a particularly nasty bear attack, which resulted in the death of one visitor and the injury of three others. Distressing incidents like these remind us to be vigilant in these remote wilderness areas.

Family activities

BC Parks offers interpretative programs in the summer, including walks, talks in the amphitheatre, and presentations. There is a children's play area and horseshoes. The campground and access road are pleasant areas to cycle around (cycling and animals are not permitted on the boardwalk).

Activities adjacent to the campground

As anyone who has travelled the Alaska Highway knows, activities are few and far between. If you like the wide open road and untouched scenery, you are onto a winner; if not, you should sojourn elsewhere. The only other activity I found while staying at Liard River Hotsprings was people-watching at the funky little café across the street, which seemed to attract its fair share of life's rich characters. If you visit this café, check out the photographs of the hot springs taken during the winter.

Summary

This campground made me want to write a long, rambling, love letter to BC Parks, telling them how wonderful they were to provide these facilities. I have extremely affectionate memories of the one time I was lucky enough to stay here. We went to the hot pools at 7:00 a.m., before most people were up and as a thunderstorm was passing, and sat in the hot waters watching the lightning as the cold rain fell into the warm pools. After the relaxing experience, we took our clean glowing bodies to breakfast at the little restaurant across the road from the campsite. It was a perfect start to the day. Liard River Hotsprings is well worth a visit, and unlike many of the commercially developed hot springs in the south of the province, it remains a totally natural environment. This is one of my favourite provincial parks. If you get a chance to visit, do not wait—GO!

17. Lakelse Lake

For those who crave mountain views; cool, clear lakes; sandy beaches; and easy access to mineral hot springs, together with a campground offering all facilities, this is the place to be. I booked into this campground in mid-September, planning to stay just one night before heading to my destination in the Queen Charlotte Islands. I ended up staying four nights, as the road between Terrace and Prince Rupert was blocked by a landslide. What a perfect place to be delayed. Lakelse is a provincial park suitable for every age and every interest, with loads of activities within its boundaries and in the adjacent towns. The biggest draw for me, however, is Mount Layton Hot Springs, 3 kilometres from the park itself.

History

There are nine hot, odourless pools in the region. These pools were first discovered by the Haisla and Tsimshian people who travelled the area centuries ago. In 1904-05 a wagon road was built adjacent to the springs to supply material for the construction of a railway that was to run from Kitimat to northern B.C. During the initial railroad exploration (which never came to fruition), Bruce Johnson acquired the land and built a hotel at the hot springs in 1910. Despite the lack of rail transportation, Johnson developed a successful business around the hot springs by advertising extensively in the United States. He ultimately built a second hotel and bathhouse at the lakeside, but hard times during the Great Depression, coupled with a fire, led to the abandonment of the venture. The springs remained undeveloped until 1958, when the facilities were renovated. They subsequently changed ownership on a number of occasions and in the early 1980s were completely re-renovated under the name Mount Layton Resort. Today this is one of the most developed hot springs in the province.

Location

In the midst of the majestic old-growth forest of the Skeena River Watershed, ringed by mountains of the Kitimat Range of the Coast Mountains, and surrounded by a comprehensive range of facilities including hot springs, this is an attractive campground for all ages. The park, 24 kilometres south of Terrace on Highway 37, is a beautiful haven for the traveller. Services can be found either in Terrace or in Kitimat, 33 kilometres to the south. Mount Layton Resort has a restaurant, coffee shop, and pub.

Facilities

The 156 large, well-organized, and well-maintained gravel campsites cater to every type of recreational vehicle and are set within a forest of cedar, hemlock, and Sitka spruce. There are full facilities here, including a sani-

Lakelse Provincial Park.

station, flush toilets, and showers. There are facilities for the disabled, and reservations are accepted. This is one of the best-cared-for campgrounds that I have stayed in.

Recreational activities

Hot springs

Mount Layton Hot Springs are reputed to be the hottest in Canada, with waters that are colourless, odourless, and tasteless. During the summer the hot springs are open from 10:00 a.m. to 10:00 p.m. There is one large pool at 30 degrees C (87 degrees F); a smaller, hotter pool at 41 degrees C (106 degrees F), and a "turtle" pool for children, 32 degrees C (90 degrees F), which contains large, brightly coloured plastic animals that were originally used at Expo 86 in Vancouver. The park has five waterslides. A café, restaurant, and pub are all on site and the admission price is reduced a dollar if you are staying at the provincial park. This is a wonderful place to spend the day no matter what the weather is like.

Hiking

There are not many hiking possibilities adjacent to the park, although a 2-kilometre, self-guided nature trail, the Twin Spruce Trail, offers an easy walk through the forest. When I did the trail I was surprised by the lack of interpretative signage. I later learned that walkers needed a parks brochure to read about the points of interest, so remember to collect one before you start. Larger hiking trails start from the town of Kitimat. Ask for details at the town's visitors centre.

Fishing

The fishing here is reputed to be fantastic. Both trout and Dolly Varden are frequently caught, while all five species of Pacific salmon, as well as steelhead and char, are available. In August, sockeye salmon spawn in William's Creek in the northern part of the park, and BC Parks literature boasts "world class salmon and steelhead runs." There is excellent chinook and coho fishing in the nearby Skeena and Kitimat Rivers, and the towns of Kitimat and Terrace have numerous shops dedicated to every aspect of this sport. During my visit it appeared 90 percent of the other campers were there to fish.

Boating

There is a paved, double boat launch in the park at Furlong Bay Campground. Power boating, canoeing, water-skiing, and windsurfing are all popular activities.

Wildlife viewing

Mammals that inhabit the region include moose, wolves, coyotes, cougars, and black bears. The famous Kermode bear—a white-coloured black bear—is also native to the region but is rarely seen, except as an emblem on municipal property in Terrace. Over 100 species of birds have been identified here. In the Tsimshian language, *lakelse* means "freshwater mussel," so expect to find some of these while exploring the waters of the lake.

Family activities

Children will adore the soft sands of the beaches in this park, and in summer the lake waters warm up to temperatures that encourage swimming. Near the beach are a change house, playground, and numerous picnic tables. Interpretative programs are offered throughout the summer and advertised on the park notice boards. Paved roads wind through the campsite for cyclists and rollerbladers.

Activities adjacent to the park

The town of Kitimat to the south offers tours of the world's largest aluminium smelter and also boasts B.C.'s oldest Sitka spruce tree. The town's information centre is open throughout the year. To the north, Terrace is famous for "fishing and bears," but offers little else for tourists. In Terrace I found a shop with a sign that read "prepared moose meat." I had never tasted moose and, thinking it could be interesting on the barbecue, I went in to buy some, only to be told by the proprietor that I had to go and kill the animal first; then he would prepare the meat...I did not attempt this.

Summary

Lakelse is a delight to visit, providing a range of activities both within its boundaries and in the surrounding area. Families with young children will find it particularly enjoyable, as indeed will anglers. It is easy to spend an entire day at the hot springs, and children (and some adults) will be entertained for hours on the waterslides and play areas available. The older generation should also appreciate the restorative waters of the springs, which are open well into the evening hours. I spent a wonderful Wednesday evening in mid-September as one of four people enjoying the hot springs. My husband and I had races down the waterslides for an hour; then the only other couple in the place, who were both over 60, confessed they were jealous of our screams and enjoyment and followed our noisy example once we vacated the slides. After this activity we retired to the pub for darts and shuffleboard, food, and drinks. Returning to the uncrowded campground at 10:00 p.m., the BC Parks representative met us at the gate, ready to collect our camping fee and ensure we were having a good time. (It reminded me of my father waiting for me to return home from a night out when I was a teenager). If you get the opportunity, stay at Lakelse—you will not regret it.

18. Kootenay National

During my first visit to Kootenay National Park I met a parks representative who told me that Kootenay was often overlooked in comparison to its well-known neighbours, with just over 1.2 million visitors a year compared to Banff's 4.7 million and Jasper's 2.2 million. For anyone who has experienced the crowds at Lake Louise or Banff in August, this can only be good news. Kootenay's 1406 square kilometres are rich in variety. It is the only park to contain both glacial peaks and cactus within its boundary, but these are not the only rewards; Radium Hot Springs, numerous gorges, waterfalls, mountains, and two major river systems (the Vermilion and the Kootenay) add to its glory, as do a host of interesting excursions for the tourist. In 1985 UNESCO designated Banff, Jasper, Yoho, and Kootenay National Parks as World Heritage Sites, officially recognizing the beauty and significance of the Rocky Mountains and forming one of the largest protected mountainous areas in the world.

History

Interpretive boards at Marble Canyon in the park detail the area's 500-million-year geological development. Human habitation is a little more contemporary. Aboriginal people have travelled, hunted, and camped in the region for over 11,000 years. They recognized the magic of the hot springs and regarded them as sacred waters, a place to cure illness and gain spiritual peace. The first registered owner of the hot springs was Roland Stuart, an Englishman who purchased 160 acres of land, including the hot springs, for $160 in the first decade of the 1900s. The government of Canada expropriated the land and springs from Stuart in 1923 and have been responsible for them ever since. Kootenay National Park was opened in 1920 and owes its birth to Highway 93, the first motor road to cross the central Canadian Rockies, which in turn led to the development of motorized tourism. The Province of B.C. gave the park to the Government of Canada in return for the road.

Location

The park encompasses land of the Continental Divide and the Columbia Valley. The west entrance is 1 kilometre north of Radium, and the park stretches along 90 kilometres of Highway 93 as it heads north. All services can be found at Radium and there is a restaurant, store, and information office at Vermilion Crossing, operated by Kootenay Park Lodge and located roughly in the centre of the park.

Facilities

Four campgrounds operate within the park's boundaries. The largest and most popular is Redstreak, which is open from early May until the end of

September and has 242 sites, including 50 with full hook-up and 38 with electricity. Flush toilets, showers, and a sani-station are available here, as are facilities for the disabled. Redstreak is my personal preference as not only does it have all amenities, but it is also possible to walk to the hot springs from here. This campground is not well signposted; you enter it by exiting the park and taking a paved road by the RCMP station in Radium on Highway 93/95. Stay here if you want easy access to the hot waters.

McLeod Meadows Campground is open from mid-May until mid-September and is 26 kilometres north of Radium between Meadow Creek and Kootenay River. It has 98 spaces, flush toilets a sani-station, but no showers. The spaces are large enough for every size of RV and are in a lightly forested area, with some of the best locations being close to the river. The third campground is Marble Canyon, open from mid-June until early September, with 61 spaces, 86 kilometres north of Radium. Set in a dense sub-alpine forest, it is the quaintest of the campgrounds and has flush toilets and a sani-station but no showers. The final campground is Dolly Varden, a winter location open from September 14 till May 7 with only basic facilities. Reservations are not taken at any campground in Kootenay National Park and there is a three dollar fee for firewood.

Recreational Activities

Hot springs

Radium Hot Springs are probably the best known of B.C.'s hot springs and among the most developed. They are also the most radioactive hot springs in Canada, but do not worry—this radioactivity is too weak to be harmful. The pools are immensely popular; over 400,000 people use the facilities each year. There are two developed open-air pools—a hot soaking pool with temperatures up to 47.7 degrees C (118 degrees F), and a cooler swimming pool, 24 metres long, with hot water cooled by creek water to 27 degrees C (81 degrees F). The smaller, hotter pool nestles into the walls of the

Radium Hot Springs pool.

cliff, and it is possible to look up to see bighorn sheep on the ledges above the pool. You can access the pools via a trail from Redstreak Campground or by vehicle. The hot springs are very popular, especially during the summer months, although when I visited in July I found that 9:00 a.m., when they first opened in the morning, was a good time to go to avoid the crowds. For those who arrive unprepared, locker rooms, showers, and swimsuit and towel rentals are all available. This is a great place for kids and fully accessible for the disabled.

Hiking

One of the joys of Kootenay Park is the number of short, easy, yet fascinating trails that can be undertaken by any age group. Amongst the most popular are: Olive Lake, a boardwalk trail with interpretative signboards and a fish-viewing platform, 13 kilometres from Radium; Paint Pots (85 kilometres north of Radium), a 1.5-kilometre trail leading to cold, iron-infested mineral springs that bubble up through the earth and stain it a deep ochre colour; and Marble Canyon, a 1-kilometre interpretative trail through an impressive narrow canyon of grey limestone that leads to a pounding waterfall (remember the camera if you do this one). There are over 200 kilometres of trails in the park, so numerous day hikes are possible in addition to overnight excursions. One of the most popular day hikes is a 10-kilometre, five-hour-return trek to Stanley Glacier through a dramatic landscape of fire and ice. Details of all these routes can be obtained from the park information centre, 3 kilometres north of Radium, or at the Vermilion Crossing Visitors Centre, 63 kilometres north of Radium.

Fishing

While it is possible to fish for brook and rainbow trout, whitefish, and Dolly Varden, most of the streams and rivers are fed by glaciers, so the water is too cold to yield high fish populations.

Boating

Only non-motorized craft are permitted on the lakes and rivers in the park.

Wildlife viewing

In addition to 179 species of birds found in the park, Kootenay is home to 5 to 10 grizzly bears, 15 to 25 black bears, 5 to 10 wolves, 50 to 75 elk, 50 to 70 moose, 100 to 140 bighorn sheep, and 250 to 300 mountain goats. I did not count them—these figures come from a 1998 publication put out by the park. The best time to see these creatures is in the early morning and at dusk.

Family activities

With no developed beach or natural waterfront, Kootenay is not a prime family location. However Redstreak Campground does provide easy access to the hot springs and pool, has an adventure playground, and offers

Follow the boardwalk and the interpretative signboards at Olive Lake.

interpretative programs in the summer, so if you have children to entertain, my advice would be to stay here. The numerous short trails scattered throughout the park are easy for children to complete, give you a break as you drive through the park, and are immensely educational.

Activities adjacent to the park

The communities of Radium and Invermere offer a number of commercial activities including golfing. Invermere is a pretty town whose main street is lined with flowers in the summer. Lake Windermere, a fifteen-minute drive south of Kootenay National Park, has two lovely beaches and relatively warm waters, easily accessible from James Chabot Provincial Park (no camping).

Summary

For me there are two sides to Kootenay National Park. The southern portion near Radium is busy and somewhat commercialized. During the summer months it is crowded as tourists congregate around the therapeutic waters of the hot springs. The other side of Kootenay is its vast expanse away from the hot waters, which provides a cornucopia of things to see and do. It is easy to spend two to three days travelling slowly through the park, exploring its natural wonders.

For those who want access to the hot springs but wish to retire to a quiet, small campground in the evenings, Dry Gulch Provincial Park is an interesting option. Five kilometres south of Radium on Highway 93/95, this little-known haven has 26 tranquil sites that to my eye are superior to those at Redstreak. There are no showers or hook-ups.

19. Whiteswan Lake

Ever had a fantasy about being a logging truck driver, bouncing along dirt roads miles from anywhere, surrounded by wilderness and with only a moose or two to get in your path? The road to Whiteswan can fulfil these trucking fantasies. This provincial park is off the beaten track and involves a journey of 18 kilometres along a rough gravel road before you reach the park entrance. Part of this road runs high above Lussier Creek and can be quite an adventure, especially as it is regularly used by logging trucks, is characterized by potholes, and narrows to one lane in places. If you can cope with the journey (our small Mazda 323 did, with the only problem being a mud-caked car upon arrival at the campground), then the camping experience—which includes two clear mountain lakes, abundant wildlife, first-rate fishing, and natural hot springs—will be your well-earned reward. It seems to me the hot springs have been put there as a treat for those who have successfully navigated the route.

History

Five thousand years ago the Ktunaxa people used Whiteswan Lake as a seasonal hunting camp. During the 1800s and early 1900s explorers, trappers, prospectors, and guides worked in the region. Today logging is the prime activity, as you will see on your journey to the park.

Location

Whiteswan Lake is located in the Kootenay Range of the Rocky Mountains, off Highway 93/95 east of Canal Flats. An 18-kilometre gravel road leads to the park entrance, with the most distant campground being 34 kilometres from the main highway. You will find a store and restaurant at Canal Flats, while more comprehensive services are farther afield at Invermere to the north.

Facilities

There are four campgrounds to choose from, each providing a different type of camping adventure. Alces Lake is located 21 kilometres from the highway and has some superb sites, many overlooking the lake, all large and secluded, some with tent pads. As with all the campgrounds at Whiteswan, only the basic facilities are provided (wood, water, fire pit, pit toilet, picnic table). A sani-station is located here. The second campground is Packrat Point, 24 kilometres from the highway, in an area of dark, dense forest with just 16 spots. There are a number of pull-through sites. I found the sites not as agreeable as at Alces Lake, but they are nearer the boat launch. A third campground is at Inlet Creek, 28 kilometres from the paved road. This is the most undesirable location as the campsites are in a large gravel parking area with little privacy. Probably the best campground is Home Basin, 34 kilometres from the highway. Be warned: the road

View from Home Basin Campground at Whiteswan Provicial Park.

between Inlet Creek and Home Basin does decline—watch out for lots of bumps and potholes—but it is still navigable with an RV. With 37 large, private spaces in a lightly forested area, some overlooking the water's edge, this is a wonderful place to spend time. One space at Home Basin is reserved until 6:00 p.m. for disabled campers, and the campground hosts are also located here. When I visited, the hosts had colourful planters full of bedding plants at the entrance to their site, making it very inviting.

Recreational Activities

Hot springs

The Lussier Hot Springs are located at the entrance of the park, 18 kilometres from the main highway. A five-minute walk leads from a parking lot and change house/pit toilet to the pools, which are adjacent to the cool rushing waters of Lussier Creek. The hottest pool is approximately five metres in diameter and half a metre deep, with a gravel floor. It has a slight smell of sulphur, not too severe, and can reach temperatures of 43.4 degrees C (110 degrees F). Several smaller pools are nearer the waters of the river, each cooler than the one above it. When the river is high, those pools closest take in the river waters so are not that warm. We visited these pools as heavy rain poured down in June and really appreciated their warm offerings following the bumpy journey. It is quite a beautiful location; the waters of the Lussier are a lovely milky-blue colour and provide a contrast to the grey rock and dark green of the surrounding vegetation. We were lucky enough to have the place to ourselves, but I can imagine that with more than ten people it may feel crowded.

Follow the trail to the Lussier Hot Springs shown above.

Hiking

A hiking trail (16 kilometres return) follows the north shore of Whiteswan Lake from Home Basin to Alces Lake and takes about five hours to complete. For those who desire more challenging routes, visit Top of the World Provincial Park by travelling 30 kilometres along a gravel road from a signposted turnoff just before Alces Lake Campground. This is an alpine wilderness park of considerable beauty. A popular hike here is a two-hour trail along the Lussier River to Fish Lake.

Fishing

Whiteswan Lake Provincial Park forms part of the Rocky Mountain Triangle, three parks reputed to have some of the best fishing in the province. The other two are Premier Lake (see Chapter 6) and Top of the World Provincial Park (Fish Lake). Both Alces and Whiteswan Lakes have excellent fishing for rainbow trout (only fly fishing is allowed in Alces Lake), which can be seen spawning in May and June in Inlet and Outlet Creeks. The lakes are stocked annually.

Boating

There are boat launches at Packrat Point and Home Basin Campgrounds. Only electric motors are permitted on Alces Lake, which is much smaller than Whiteswan.

Wildlife viewing

There are opportunities to view wildlife such as mountain goats, bighorn sheep, and moose (*Alces* is Latin for "moose"). Bird life includes loons, red-necked grebes, belted kingfishers, herons, golden eagles, and bald eagles.

Family activities

This is an adult campground, geared to hot springs, boating, and fishing. It is possible to swim from a beach at the north end of Whiteswan Lake, but there are no formal programs or play areas for children. At Home Basin there is an historic cabin with displays and information boards.

Activities adjacent to the park

As mentioned above, Top of the World Provincial Park and Premier Provincial Park are both within easy reach of Whiteswan. The nearby town of Kimberley is a quaint place to visit. It has adopted a Bavarian theme, so the high street is full of restaurants playing accordion music and serving veal schnitzel and apple strudel. The high street is also home to the world's largest cuckoo clock, though a yodeller rather than a bird pops out on the hour (and when tourists ply it with 25 cents).

Summary

Whiteswan provides an adult camping experience, perfect for the angler, kayaker, and camper who does not require organized entertainment. Its location, high in the Rocky Mountains, promises a true get-away-from-it-all treat. I do not recommend this campground for anyone with young children or who prefers more commercialized camping, but for all others it is a real find. In contrast to the other campgrounds recommended in this section, it offers a much less commercialized hot-springs adventure.

Additional Recommendations

Kokanee Creek See Chapter 2. Ainsworth Hot Springs are a short drive north of Kokanee Creek Provincial Park.

Blanket Creek See Chapter 5. Nakusp Hot Springs are about an hour south of Blanket Creek.

THE BEST "HIDDEN GEM" CAMPGROUNDS

One of the constant cries of seasoned campers is that their favourite places have become too popular in recent years. This section is for these people. The campgrounds I have included are ones that for some reason do not seem to be as popular as others, yet in my opinion justify exploration.

Kentucky-Alleyne is neither too big nor too small, can be easily reached from Vancouver or the Okanagan, and is set in wonderful undulating countryside. It is a campground that never feels crowded, where accommodation is rarely a problem (except on long weekends) and where visitors can relax beside two tranquil lakes. Blanket Creek, south of Revelstoke, is not only a delightful place to stop, but is also a base from which to plan a vacation touring the centre of the province. Syringa is a campground in the Kootenays that has something for all the family and is receiving more visitors year by year. Finally, I describe Fintry Provincial Park as a hidden gem because it is relatively new and therefore few know of its existence. In ten years this will not be the case. Many of the campgrounds in this chapter are known to the locals and are therefore busy at weekends (sometimes just in the day-use areas), but the rest of us should explore them more.

20. Kentucky-Alleyne

I adore this quiet, away-from-it-all provincial park with a slightly "cowboy" feel. Unlike other parks in the busy area south of Route 1, Kentucky-Alleyne is not on a major highway and therefore is not too well known or popular. It is located in the heart of cattle country in a stunningly beautiful area of undulating hills and grasslands surrounded by forests of pine and fir, a topography that is the result of heavy glaciation during the Pleistocene Age (or so I learned from reading the park's notice board). One of its big advantages for me (and for other residents of the Lower Mainland) is that it is less than four hours' drive from Vancouver, so provides an idyllic weekend getaway in the summer.

History

The area has a history of ranching but owes much of its recent development to the growth in popularity of fishing—there are approximately 150 lakes in the region. Prior to European settlement, the land near Merritt was the border between territories of two First Nations communities, the Nlaka'pamux of the Fraser and Thompson Rivers, and the Okanagan. The park was established in 1981 to preserve an area of lower elevation grassland and coniferous forest on the Thompson Plateau.

Location

The 144-hectare park between Kentucky and Alleyne Lakes is found east off Highway 5A, 55 kilometres north of Princeton and 38 kilometres south of Merritt (where the nearest services are located). A good 3-kilometre gravel road, which is quite twisting in places but navigable for all RVs, leads to the campground. There is another gravel access road from Highway 97C, but it is quicker to drive the route off Highway 5A.

Both lakes offer camping spots and the water is very warm in the summer.

Facilities

There are 63 camping spots available in the park. While not all the sites have the advantage of vegetation to afford privacy, they are well spaced and are suitable for every recreational vehicle, and all have views of the water. A few lucky campers even have direct access to the lake. Facilities are the basic ones found in BC Parks (wood, water, pit toilets, fire pit, picnic tables). For those who want to avoid other campers and do not mind a bumpy road, four detached camping spots at the far end of Alleyne Lake provide a great retreat.

Recreational Activities

Hiking

A 4-kilometre hiking trail circling Kentucky Lake is an easy stroll for every age group and provides access in certain places to the water's edge and fishing spots away from the campground (look out for the beaver lodge). There are a number of other trails; you can walk along the gravel roads leading to the four detached camping sites, for example, and over fields (watch out for the No Trespassing signs).

Fishing

This place is an angler's delight for fishing enthusiasts of any age. One of the smaller lakes in the park has been designated a "children's only" lake. In 1991 it was stocked with 1000 fingerling trout to provide a special fishing opportunity for children. Both Kentucky and Alleyne Lakes have good fishing for rainbow trout, and if you get bored on these there are over 100 other lakes in the immediate area to try. When I last visited, researchers from the University of British Columbia were conducting a

These campers are so close to the lake, they could back right in.

study in the park, asking anglers to document the size of their catch...and they expected to get the truth?!

Boating

Tranquillity is the order of the day here. Powerboats are not permitted on either of the lakes, so both are great for paddling.

Family activities

The sparkling, azure-blue waters of Kentucky and Alleyne Lakes are good for swimming (although I found them a bit weedy in places), canoeing, and sunbathing. The gravel roads through the park appeal to mountain bikers. One of the unique features of this park is the colour it displays at different times of the year. A visit in May features pastel green hillsides, while in August these hillsides are brown and parched. In the fall the colours are more vivid again. If you visit in September you may experience a piece of cowboy history as the Douglas Lake Ranch conducts its annual cattle drive through the park from the summer range to the home ranch.

Activities adjacent to the park

The town of Merritt has adopted the slogan "A lake a day as long as you stay" and boasts trout and salmon fishing as well as playing up its location in the heart of cattle country. These attributes are featured in displays at the visitors centre, located in a huge log building with red roof. The centre also houses a gift shop and snack bar.

For those who choose not to cook breakfast over an open fire, the Coldwater Hotel in Merritt provides a good start to the day. Built in 1908 for $6000, it was regarded as one of the finest hotels in B.C.'s Interior. Breakfasts served during the weekend I visited involved copious quantities of good food and drew an interesting mix of colourful locals, staff, and tourists. The hotel is a great place for people-watching.

Summary

One of my best memories of this park is of the sunsets. During our first visit we cooked dinner and afterwards sat and watched the sun go down and the sky turn to a blazing red and orange. The lake was still, but ospreys circled above and occasionally dived into the waters. It was a perfect end to a day in which we had been lucky enough to find the only available camping space at 2:00 p.m. on the hot Labour Day weekend and had then enjoyed a walk along the shady trail and two hours of swimming and sunbathing in the refreshing lake waters. This park is a favourite of mine as it is within easy access of the Lower Mainland, is essentially uncommercialized, and does not offer a sanitized camping experience. When I yearn to get away from my Vancouver home and do not want the hassle of a ferry line-up, I head for Kentucky-Alleyne. See you there.

21. Blanket Creek

Numerous guidebooks have been written about B.C.—*Adventuring in BC*, *The BC Handbook*, *Off the Beaten Track in Western Canada*, *Western Canada Travel Guide* to name but a few—yet none of them mention Blanket Creek Provincial Park, not even in passing. BC Parks currently does not offer a promotional leaflet on the park either, so there is little information on this camping spot. I suspect the locals want to keep this haven to themselves. I cannot blame them, as although there are few organized activities here, Blanket Creek is a blissful campground in a great location. This is why I class it as a hidden gem. If you want a beautiful place to relax, it delivers; alternatively if you are looking for a base from which to investigate the Rockies and Kootenays, Blanket Creek is ideally situated. After a hard day's touring, it is a great place to return to.

History

The provincial park was created in 1982 and contains the remains of the Domke homestead, one of the few properties unaffected when the Hugh Keenleyside Dam on the Columbia River was completed in the mid-1960s, flooding the Arrow Reservoir. The original log home, dating back to the 1920s, is still standing, although when I stayed I could not find it. Most of the other brick buildings have been dismantled, leaving only a pool and a rock well.

Location

Situated in the midst of the superb, snow-capped vistas of the Monashee and Selkirk Ranges, this 316-hectare provincial park is on the banks of Upper Arrow Lake at the point where Blanket Creek enters the Columbia River. It is 25 kilometres south of Revelstoke on Highway 23. The nearest services are at Revelstoke to the north or Nakusp to the south. A good paved but steep road leads from the highway to the park entrance.

*Blanket Creek
is the locals' secret hideaway.*

Facilities

If your ideal camping spot is amongst vegetation in a not-too-big, not-too-small campground with complete privacy and mountain views, then this is the place to be. There are 64 well-positioned sites suitable for every size of RV. Some are adjacent to overgrown meadows, while others are amongst the trees. There are flush and pit toilets but no sani-station nor access for the disabled. Reservations are accepted.

Recreational Activities

Hiking

There are no serious hikes adjacent to the campground. A number of small, easy trails ribbon through the campground and lead to the reservoir, a small circular lagoon, and a waterfall. A five-minute walk along the Old South Road takes campers to beautiful, azure, 12-metre Sutherland Falls. Take care, as sections of this trail are beginning to erode.

Fishing

Fishing in the creek yields Dolly Varden, rainbow trout, and kokanee. Watch for kokanee spawning in the northern reaches of the creek in late September/October. The reservoir contains Gerrard trout, kokanee, ling cod, walleye pike, and sturgeon to name but a few.

Sutherland Falls is just a short walk away.

Boating

There is no boat launch at Blanket Creek, but one is available if you travel 23 kilometres south to Shelter Bay Provincial Park, which also has camping but not such attractive sites, or to lovely Martha Creek Provincial Park, 5 kilometres north of Revelstoke on Highway 23. The reservoir is easily accessible to people with canoes and kayaks, who will not have a problem portaging their crafts to the waters.

Family activities

One of the biggest draws at this forested provincial park must be its circular, artificial lagoon. A sandy beach with numerous picnic tables rings its warm waters, and a grassed area to picnic on stretches off from the sand. This is a perfect place for kids. Adjacent to the day-use parking lot is a grassy area with volleyball nets, numerous marmot holes, and swings. If you decide to head for the cooler waters of the lake rather than the lagoon, be aware of the steep drop-off.

Activities adjacent to the park

Campers who choose this location as a base have a wealth of activities to pursue. The town of Revelstoke has recently responded to the demands of tourism by developing a beautiful downtown core to wander around, with people-watching and other outdoor entertainment in the summer months. I spent a wonderful evening here a few years ago, celebrating my third wedding anniversary dancing to a live jazz band at Grizzly Plaza in the warm evening temperatures. The town has a railway museum, art gallery, piano museum, and golf course. One of my most memorable excursions from Blanket Creek was a visit to the Revelstoke Dam, five minutes north of Revelstoke on Highway 23. This is one of North America's most modern hydroelectric developments. Tourists are taken up to the top of the structure to look out over the 175 metres of concrete wall.

For those who want to explore Canada's national parks, both Glacier and Revelstoke are within easy reach of Revelstoke. If you decide to travel south on Highway 23, a twenty-minute free ferry ride from Shelter Bay to Galena Bay awaits. You'll have great mountain views as you glide across the waters, so remember the camera. From Galena Bay it is only a 40-minute drive to the town of Nakusp (an Okanagan word meaning "closed in"). One of the biggest attractions here are the hot springs, just north of the town, 12 kilometres along a good gravel road that is signposted from the highway. There are two beautiful, commercial, yet not overdeveloped pools where you can sit in the therapeutic hot waters and look up to the snow-capped mountains. These are the only community-owned hot springs in B.C. Nakusp also has boating, golfing, and cycling opportunities.

Summary

This is a marvellous area of the world to explore or relax in. The mountainous scenery together with the tranquil, clear blue waters of the reservoir (which stretches an amazing 230 kilometres south into Washington state) offer the perfect environment for a camping vacation. If you are visiting in July or August and want to escape the crowds, my advice is to head south on Highway 23, where even in the height of summer the roads remain quiet. I stayed at Blanket Creek in early June, when we were one of only four camping parties in the park, so it felt like the entire place was ours. If you are looking for a campground where you can spend time and from which you can explore the surrounding Rockies, this is the place to be.

22. Syringa Creek

When the campground host returns to the same campground each year and spends not one but three months giving advice and information to tourists, you know this provincial park is special. Syringa Creek, situated on the eastern arm of Lower Arrow Lake below the Norns Range of the Columbia Mountains, is a location I would not mind living in for the entire summer. It is relatively quiet, not too large, has easy access to services, and contains fantastic scenery, a beach, and excellent camping sites. There is little not to like about this provincial park, which is named after the Syringa or mock orange, a regional white-flowered shrub that blooms in the early spring and emits an aroma similar to that of the fruit.

History

The region is rich in Doukhobor history as this group of pacifist Russians began settling in the region from the early 1900s. They founded more than 24 small villages, including Robson, near Syringa, and they built sawmills, planted orchards, developed jam factories, and formed one of the most successful communal enterprises in North America. You can learn about this history when you visit the museum in Castlegar. In the 1960s the area was changed by the construction of the Hugh Keenleyside Dam, south of the park, which created Arrow Lake from a section of the Columbia River (see below).

"Bugs" and Jackie, the hosts at Syringa Creek when I visited.

Location

You reach the campground by turning off Highway 3A just north of Castlegar and heading 19 kilometres on a paved road along Arrow Lake. All services are available in Castlegar, while the nearby Syringa Park Marina and store have more limited supplies.

Facilities

All 60 of the camping spaces here are good, and some have the added advantage that they overlook the water. Others are close to a grassy meadow. All are large, private, and shaded by a forest of red cedar, western larch, and ponderosa pine that

Some campsites overlook the water.

easily accommodates the biggest RV. The park is wheelchair accessible, has flush and pit toilets (but no showers), and accepted reservations for the first time in 1998.

Recreational Activities

Hiking

Two pleasant, easy trails with viewpoints of the water lead from the campground. The first is the Syringa Trail (3.3 kilometres), the second the Yellowpine Trail (2.6 kilometres). From both of these routes you might see deer or bighorn sheep. The paved road from Castlegar ends at the provincial park, but a generally good gravel road, Deer Park Road, carries on to Deer Park, where you can walk to a pretty waterfall (one hour return). A map at the campground host's site details this route. The gravel road reveals lovely views of the lake and is good for mountain bikers.

Fishing

The Arrow Lake waterway extends from north of Revelstoke into Washington state, a distance of over 230 kilometres. There is excellent fishing for kokanee, Gerrard trout, Dolly Varden, ling cod, walleye, and sturgeon.

Boating

The only boat launch in the area is at the provincial park, and water-skiing and boating are popular pursuits. As the lake is so huge, there is plenty of room for everyone.

Family activities

The beach's biggest disadvantage is that it is pebbly and rocky and therefore not suitable for sandcastles (rock castles may be an option though) or for a relaxing sunbathe. It does, however, extend well beyond the park's boundaries, so it is possible to search for areas that are more sandy than stony, and you can walk for hours along the lakeshore. Wildflowers grow amongst the rocks and pebbles on the beach. A large grassy area with playground extends out from the beach and is perfect for ball games or sunbathing. When I visited, a group of Scouts were running wild, having water fights with plastic detergent bottles and thoroughly enjoying the vast expanse of flat ground. BC Parks warns that at certain times the beach can become quite windy. The paved roads of the campground are great for cycling or rollerblading. A day-use area with beach, picnic tables, and toilets is located a little way away from the campground, and interpretative programs are offered in the summer months at the park's amphitheatre.

Activities adjacent to the park

As mentioned above, a heritage museum near the airport in Castlegar details the town's Doukhobor culture and is well worth a visit. There is another museum located in the town's old railway station as well. Castlegar

Wide open fields, lots of beach, and superb views make this a great spot!

offers opportunities for golf, and if the weather is bad there is a 25-metre pool, hot pool, and gym to enjoy. For an informative excursion visit the Hugh Keenleyside Dam, which offers daily tours from May to September and is located 1 kilometre from Robson. Completed in 1965, the concrete structure controls 3,650,000 hectares of drainage area and has one of western Canada's few navigation locks, which can lift river craft 23 metres. The waterway is also used to transport logs. It's well worth a visit.

Summary

I see this campground as a hidden gem because there is something for everyone here; children love the pebbled beach and massive playing field, and adults adore the quiet, shady camping spots with superb views. Few guidebooks or information leaflets give more than passing mention to the park, leading me to believe that only a few people are aware of it, although this is obviously changing as the park has decided to accept reservations. I have not had the opportunity to spend the night here, but did spend an extremely informative few hours with Jackie, the campground host, who filled me in on everything there is to know about Syringa and the various activities it offers. She made me realize a week here would not be long enough to fully appreciate its numerous attributes. Jackie also gave me what is probably the best piece of information: mosquitoes are never a serious problem here as the winds ensure they do not hang around biting for long. So get the family packed and set off for a bug-free holiday at this wonderful place.

Kootenay Lake, looking towards Syringa Creek Campground.

23. Fintry

Although I describe Fintry as a hidden gem, I know it will not remain so for long, partly because it is situated on immensely popular Okanagan Lake and partly because it is in easy reach of many B.C. campers. Indeed, I am already aware that during July and August space is at a premium. The reason I can justify listing it as a hidden gem now is that it was only established in 1996 and is still relatively unknown to many seasoned campers. Unlike the other popular provincial parks in the area (e.g., Okanagan Lake, Bear Creek), this haven is yet to be explored by the masses. To me it is also less commercialized than other nearby parks; there is something of an unfinished feel about Fintry that adds to its charm. If you want quiet camping in the Okanagan, Fintry is the place to find it.

History

The park is a heritage site occupying the former Fintry estate. In the 1800s the Hudson's Bay Company fur brigade trails crossed the area, which at this time was the transportation hub of the valley. A fleet of fishing boats operated from a ferry wharf that is still in existence (although unused) today. In 1919 James Cameron, originally from Scotland, purchased the land and named it Fintry. He built several barns, a manor house, caretakers' houses, and outbuildings that are now in various states of disrepair within the park's boundaries. The land was acquired by BC Parks a few years ago and opened for the first time to campers in 1996.

Location

The 360-hectare park is located on Westside Road (Highway 97) at the side of Okanagan Lake, 34 kilometres from Kelowna, which has all services.

This grand circular barn is one of the more unique buildings located within the park boundary.

Campsites are in a large grassy area beside the lake.

Eight kilometres of good paved road lead to the campground and a small community (no services).

Facilities

The 50 camping spaces are set in a large grassy area with a sparse covering of ponderosa pine, Douglas fir, and birch. There is insufficient vegetation to make them totally private, but they are large and well spaced. The ones with views of the lake are generally the best. There are flush and pit toilets but no sani-station, showers, or disabled access. Reservations are accepted.

Recreational Activities

Hiking

While there are few structured hiking trails, a number of delightful tracks and lanes wind through the campground. When I visited, some of these were overgrown while others were obviously old farming tracks. Uncharacteristically for BC Parks, there was no map at the park entrance to guide my wanderings. This lack of signage meant it was quite an adventure, following routes and not knowing where they would lead. I discovered old barns, disused buildings, and an eagle's nest. I expect BC Parks will upgrade these routes in the future, but at the moment it is fun (and safe) to explore them without maps. Many are ideal for mountain bikes and children.

Fishing

Fishing in Okanagan Lake can yield carp, burbot, kokanee, Rocky Mountain whitefish, and large rainbow trout. The waters are clear and from the beach you can watch fish leaping for flies.

Boating

There is no boat launch at Fintry. The nearest one is at Bear Creek Provincial Park, 25 kilometres to the south.

Family activities

I can imagine this would be a great place for anyone with children. There is a long, narrow, safe pebble/sandy beach (the more sandy area is near the day-use area) along the lakeshore that grants access to the clear blue waters. Shorts Creek passes through the park and creates a series of waterfalls and deep, cool pools. If you walk along the creek you will see the remains of an old suspension bridge, as well as disused irrigation and power-generating systems. Be warned that sections of this trail are quite narrow and steep. BC Parks currently does not offer interpretative programs here, but I will not be surprised if this alters in a few years. While resting by the lake, make sure you keep an eye out for Ogopogo— the Loch Ness Monster of Lake Okanagan.

Activities adjacent to the park

Bear Creek Provincial Park, an hour's drive south, has some wonderful hiking trails and a gorgeous beach to explore (see Chapter 1). The town of Kelowna has all services and numerous tourist activities, as does Vernon. One of the best day trips in the region is a visit to the O'Keefe Ranch, 12 kilometres north of Vernon. This restored 1880s ranch has many renovated

The beach at Fintry is long and inviting.

heritage buildings, farm animals, a huge model railway display, and tours of the old mansion house. It's a bit commercialized but good fun.

Summary

I visited this campground in early May, when it was not properly open. Many of the buildings were overgrown, but signs stated they were in the process of being renovated by the B.C. Environmental Youth Team in conjunction with BC Parks. As I wandered the old estate, breathing in the strong pine smell, I kept discovering things: abandoned orchards, overgrown flowerbeds, a rusty plough, a deserted boathouse complete with brick fireplace, tree-lined gravel lanes, and circular barns. I only stayed four hours but could have spent the next four days exploring the park. I was the only visitor—it was just like entering The Secret Garden or a land that time forgot. Fintry is full of history, which is still being drawn out. For example, the old manor house near the campground, like many of the buildings, is impressive but in need of renovation, and I hope BC Parks has the money to fully restore this paradise. Visit this hidden gem soon, as I predict it will not remain undiscovered for long.

Additional Recommendations

Paarens Beach/Sowchea See Chapter 6.
Jimsmith Lake (Rockies) This is a relatively small campground with only 28 spaces. The day-use area is popular with locals but quietens in the evening. Great beach and warm lake.
Kleanza Creek (North by Northwest) A scenic campground close to a babbling river with 21 shaded camping spots and a chance to pan for gold.
Martha Creek (High Country) The 25 camping spaces here all have beautiful views, adjacent to the Revelstoke Reservoir.
Exchamsiks River (North by Northwest) Camp in old-growth forest on the banks of an azure, fast-flowing river. Relax, unwind, and gaze in awe at the scenery.

THE BEST CAMPGROUNDS TO KISS

A number of guidebooks based on the theme of "The Best Places to Kiss" have been published over the last ten years. They tend to regard $300-a-night bed and breakfast accommodation or mountaintops accessible only by renting a private helicopter as the most suitable places for people to declare affection for one another. Although the premise for this chapter has been taken from these popular texts, my recommendations do not require this kind of expenditure, but can be just as romantic. The four campgrounds detailed in this section—Naikoon, Muncho Lake, Premier Lake, and Paarens Beach—are not the most accessible. They are reached by gravel roads or ferries, or are located far in the north of the province where few tourists venture. Romantics must be dedicated to search them out, but will be amply rewarded when they have done so.

Naikoon, the only provincial park on the Queen Charlotte Islands, is an expanse of beachfront, often shrouded in mist. While temperatures here are not high, even in the summer, the scenery compensates in a way that is totally unique to B.C. Over 100 kilometres of beach with pounding sea provides the idyllic backdrop for lovers who want to be by themselves in a pristine seascape. Similarly Muncho Lake, high on the Alaska Highway, does not have the baking heat of campgrounds in the Okanagan but does have spectacular views and great wildlife viewing opportunities. Premier Lake Provincial Park is one of the less-developed campgrounds in the Rockies, yet has one of the most spectacular settings, offering what I deem to be an adult camping experience. Finally, Paarens Beach and Sowchea are two adjacent campgrounds on massive Stuart Lake. I believe anyone who sits on the beach here as the sun sinks will have a romantic experience.

24. Naikoon

For me the word Naikoon conjures up images of a beautiful, isolated, stormswept landscape, an endless expanse of beach, a roaring ocean, thick early-morning mists, everchanging sand dunes, wind, and...an unrelenting drizzle. On the largest of the Queen Charlotte Islands, this provincial park must rank along with Wells Gray, Mount Robson, and Strathcona as one of the jewels in the BC Parks crown. It is also one of the most remote, wildest, wettest (126 centimetres of rain a year), and (during the summer months) coldest (average daily August temperature is 17 degrees C). My advice for anyone considering a vacation here is to go, but go prepared. Invest in Gore-tex beforehand, anticipate the need for lots of warming cuddles, and do not expect to return home with a suntan. Despite this warning, Naikoon is a real gem—magnificent, huge, remote, and romantic. Crowds are not going to be a concern here, and if you seek adventure in the great outdoors, this is the place to be. (Note: Watch for Dennis Horwood's *Haida Gwai: A Place to Be* (Publication date May 2000)—a perfect book companion for the "Charlottes."

History

Naikoon means "long nose" and is derived from the Haida name *Nai-kun*. The Haida Nation inhabited these islands, which they called Haida Gwaii, for centuries before the first Europeans travelled to the area in the 1700s. The Spanish explorer Juan Perez arrived in 1774, followed by the British explorer Captain George Dixon, who named the islands the Queen Charlottes, thirteen years later. At that time it was estimated 7000 Haida populated the area; by 1915 the population had dropped to 600 after white settlers introduced smallpox, tuberculosis, and other diseases for

There are beautiful beaches and hardly any people at Naikoon.

*Agate Beach Campground shelter provides a place to hang
your wet clothes to dry after a rain shower.*

which the Haida had no resistance. Today the Haida (approximately 1350
people) make up one sixth of the Islands' population, and many members
of the nation are world renowned for their carving and artistic abilities.

Location

This 72,641-hectare park covers almost the entire northeast corner of
Graham Island, the largest of the Queen Charlotte Islands. It is situated
on the Argonaut Plain, a landscape formed as the melting glaciers retreated
at the end of the last ice age. Its topography is therefore the work of
glacial deposits and does not rise above 150 metres at its highest point.
No up-hill hikes here! The Queen Charlotte Islands include some 200
islands, most of them small and uninhabited. To reach the provincial park
from the mainland, campers must take a ferry (six-hour journey) from
Prince Rupert or a plane from Prince Rupert or Vancouver. BC Ferries
increases the number of sailings offered in July and August, so it is easier
to arrange a trip to Naikoon in those months than in the shoulder season
or winter when the ferries do not operate daily. (Ferry reservations are
strongly recommended). When you reach Graham Island, Naikoon is to
the north on Highway 16.

Facilities

There are two campgrounds. Misty Meadows is located near Tlell, 42
kilometres north of Skidegate on Highway 16, and Agate Beach is 26
kilometres northeast of Masset on a secondary road. The 43 sites at Agate
Beach are close to the ocean and somewhat exposed. In contrast, the 30
at Misty Meadows are situated under pine trees. Neither site has a sani-
station or flush toilets. Both campsites have basic facilities (pit toilets,
water, wood, fire pit, picnic tables) and there is limited disabled access. My
preference is to stay at Misty Meadows as the sites are more sheltered,
there are trees in which to secure tarps, and in 1998 some wonderful BC

The Dunes Trail takes you through a rainforest. In places you will find a felt covered, wooden pathway keeping you up of the forest floor.

Parks worker had ensured colourful, flower-filled baskets hung from the entrance of each site. Wilderness camping is permitted throughout the park, and there are three wilderness shelters: two located along East Beach near the mouths of the Cape Ball and Oeanda Rivers, and one at Fife Point. The park headquarters are located at the southeast entrance near Tlell on Highway 16. Anyone considering adventuring here should collect information brochures, especially if you are planning to take the longer hikes. Services are available in the towns of Tlell, Port Clements, Masset, and Queen Charlotte City.

Recreational activities

Hiking

Hiking is the primary recreational activity in this park. You can spend hours wandering over 100 kilometres of everchanging beaches, looking for shells, clams, sea agates, and shipwreck debris. In addition to these casual strolls, a number of trails have been developed from the two campgrounds. From the Tow Hill Parking Area near Agate Beach in the north of the park it is possible to follow the Hiellen River north to a view of a blow hole (Blow Hole Trail). Or you can take the one-hour-return Tow Hill Trail for fantastic views of the Argonaut Plain and a taste of salt air. Wooden boards covered with non-slip felt form the path. You can get to the north beach by crossing a small bridge over the Hiellen River. Here you can while away many hours beachcombing and exploring the coastline. We walked to the shipwreck of the *Kelly Rose* (three hours return) and were the only people on the beach. Finally, the Cape Fife Loop Trail leads hikers on a 21-kilometre walk through coastal rain forest and bogs to a lookout.

Hike to the wreck of the Pesuta *(top) or follow the Blow Hole Trail.*

From Misty Meadows Campground there is a trail leading to the beach (Dunes Trail); a 10-kilometre-return walk to the wreck of the *Pesuta* (a ship built in 1919 that once hauled timber but which ran aground in 1928), which takes you through old-growth forest and along the river to the ocean; and a major 94-kilometre (one way) hike along the length of East Beach. Individuals considering this last trek need to be well prepared and must register with the RCMP, obtain tidal timetables so they know when it's safe to cross the many tributaries, and ensure they have plenty of fresh water.

Fishing

Fish are plentiful in and around Naikoon. The Tlell River is renowned for steelhead and coho runs, while cutthroat trout and Dolly Varden are common in the streams that run through the park. Cutthroat trout can also be caught in Mayer Lake, which is a wonderful picnic spot. Fishing trips can be organized from Masset.

Wildlife viewing

There is a wealth of wildlife to be observed at Naikoon. Non-native species include elk, blacktail deer (which are everywhere), racoons, red squirrels, beavers, and muskrats. Native species such as black bears and river otters are found on the land, and dolphins, orcas, porpoises, sea lions, and seals in the waters. Ornithologists love the area for observing migrating birds including sandhill cranes, cormorants, gulls, pigeon guillemots, oystercatchers, loons, and plovers. The Queen Charlotte Islands boast the second-highest eagle density in the world.

Family activities

Naikoon is not a campground oriented to family activities, although older children who like outdoor pursuits may enjoy it. The cooler temperatures and damp climate mean that sandcastle construction is not a preferred activity, even though the beaches are fantastic.

Activities adjacent to the park

Masset is the largest community in the Charlottes and has the most services. At Old Masset, 2 kilometres north of Masset and at one time the largest Haida village on the islands, there are three ancient Haida township sites complete with totem poles. A visitors centre for Gwaii Haanas (South Moresby National Park) is located in Queen Charlotte City and is well worth a visit, while Pure Lake Provincial Park, south of Masset, offers an easy two-hour hike around a lake away from the sea breeze.

Summary

My advice to anyone planning a romantic getaway to Naikoon is to take time in preparing the excursion. I tried to visit in 1995, when a rockslide closed the road between Terrace and Prince Rupert for four days and prevented me from reaching the ferry terminal. In 1998 I initially planned to visit Naikoon in June and spend three days there, but I found organizing ferry travel at this time of the year problematic, as the ferries did not sail daily. Consequently we ended up visiting at the end of August. The little cabin allocated to us by BC Ferries was gorgeous, making the overnight journey fly by. Upon arrival we found the days comparatively cool, but with a good windbreaker I was not deterred from fully investigating the magnificent park. To me the lack of people and the vast expanse of island beach were attractive and I spent hours wandering along this shoreline, a trek that is enhanced considerably if undertaken with a romantic friend you can cuddle up with against the wind. Naikoon is an effort to reach, but it is an effort you will not regret.

25. Muncho Lake

If you adore remote natural beauty, some of the most spectacular scenery in B.C. awaits you as you travel the 113 kilometres of the Alaska Highway that pass through the middle of 88,416-hectare Muncho Lake Provincial Park. The landscape here is stunning and lives in my memory as the most breathtaking section of the Alaska Highway. Expect to work the camera hard as you travel by high mountains where tectonic deformations have folded the limestone, giving these peaks a unique appearance. Brilliantly coloured wildflowers cover the hillsides, especially in June, and then there is the breathtaking jade green of Muncho Lake itself. The distinctive colour of the lake is caused by small rock fragments eroded from the valley walls by glaciers and carried by meltwater downstream to the lake. Most of the silt sinks to the bottom, but fine particles the size of flour granules remain suspended in the lake, giving it a milky appearance. These fine grains reflect and scatter the sun's rays to give the lake its brilliant blue-green colour, the sort of colour friends will not believe when you show them your holiday snaps.

History

In the dialect of the Kaska First Nation, *muncho* means "big," so Muncho Lake means "big lake." The Kaska people were the first inhabitants of this area, and Muncho Lake is presumed to have been one of their primary encampments as three ancient campsites have been identified here. European explorers, trappers, and traders started passing through the region in the late 1800s, but major development only occurred with the construction of the Alaska Highway in the 1940s. Even that has failed to spoil this remote region which, except for the occasional settlement on the Alaska Highway, remains largely undeveloped. The park was established in 1957.

Location

Set amongst some of the most beautiful, rugged, wilderness scenery in the province, Muncho Lake is located at Mile 422 of the Alaska Highway, 250 kilometres west of Fort Nelson. The provincial park is situated in the Terminal and Muskwa Ranges of the Rocky Mountains, an area noted for its classic Rocky Mountain features such as vaulted rock and alluvial fans. Services such as gas, restaurants, accommodation, and small stores are, unusually, located in the park itself in the small town of Muncho Lake.

Facilities

There are 30 campsites in two campgrounds, both on the shores of Muncho Lake. The more northerly campground, MacDonald, has fifteen spots that are quite close to the road, affording little privacy. The sound of traffic is not a tremendous problem, though, as the road does not tend to be busy. Strawberry

*Campgrounds at Muncho Lake provide basic facilities
along the Alaska Highway.*

Flats (my preference) is the more southerly location with fifteen more private spots, some of them on the waterfront. There is no sani-station and facilities are basic in both campgrounds (fire pit, wood, water, pit toilets, picnic tables). Both campgrounds can be somewhat windy and cool.

Recreational Activities

Hiking
Although there are a number of hikes in the park, the trails are not well marked, so if you are considering exploring the region by foot, ensure you get a good map. There are a number of hiking possibilities at Stone Mountain Provincial Park (see below).

Boating
The park has a boat launch at MacDonald Campground, and in the summer boaters, canoeists, kayakers, and windsurfers are all attracted to the 12-kilometre jewel of a lake whose depth varies from 2 metres to over 500 metres. The waters stay very cold all year round, so wet suits and warm clothing are advised. The lake is also subject to strong winds. A business in the community of Muncho Lake offers boat tours of the lake at certain times of the year.

Fishing
As the waters of the lake are cold, the fishing is not great, but it is possible to catch lake trout, Arctic grayling, Dolly Varden, and whitefish in the wonderfully coloured waters. You might have better luck if you fish the waters of Toad and Trout Rivers.

Wildlife viewing

There are excellent wildlife viewing opportunities. Mineral licks attract stone sheep and caribou (one of the best places to see them is near Kilometre 760, Mile 474, of the Alaska Highway. The best viewing time is at dawn or dusk in the late spring or early fall). Moose are quite common in the Toad River Valley near the park's eastern boundary, and beaver,s coyotes, mountain goats, black bears, grizzly bears, and wolves all live in and around the park. BC Parks literature states that this is one of the best areas for viewing moose and caribou, but cautions drivers to be careful when stopping abruptly to view wildlife. In 1993 five moose, eighteen stone sheep, and ten caribou road kills were reported to BC Parks staff in the region. Many more go unreported, so do use caution while driving. Bird life includes Canada geese, various ducks, loons, grebes, and gulls.

Family activities

There is little for families with young children to do in this remote area. The waters are too cold for swimming and the campground activities are geared to adults.

Activities adjacent to the park

As mentioned above, the small community of Muncho Lake provides a number of services including restaurants and a few shops. There are also a couple of tour operators offering guided access to this remote region. Stone Mountain Provincial Park, 60 kilometres southeast of Muncho Lake Park, contains the highest part of the Alaska Highway (4183 feet) within its boundaries. From this location serious hikers can tackle the five- to seven-day Wokkpash Trail. For the less ambitious, a number of shorter trails are easily accessible from Stone Mountain.

Summary

I contend that just *being* in this remote, romantic location is one of the most pleasant pastimes. Muncho Lake provides the ideal environment to unwind and relax away from urban pressures. If you seek organized activity, go somewhere else. This is a wonderful, away-from-it-all location with brilliant photographic opportunities. When I travelled the Alaska Highway in early September I saw moose, caribou, black bear, grizzly bear, and stone sheep on a number of occasions. This was a real thrill for me as normally all I see are the "watch for wildlife" signs and no animals at all. This area is reported to have fantastic wildflowers, especially in late June when orchids bloom and in July when the alpine meadows at the higher elevations are in their full glory. Lovers wishing to secure a suntan may be disappointed, as the weather here is changeable; snow flurries are not unheard of in September, and at any time of year the camping can be cool and windy, so come prepared to engage in lots of cuddling to keep warm.

26. Premier Lake

I stayed here in mid-June when the weather was good, with blue skies, warm temperatures, and no winds. The park was full of the scent of wild roses, honeysuckle, and wildflowers too numerous to name. There wasn't a mosquito in sight. Is it therefore any wonder this campground scores a 10 out of 10 for this camper? At this time of year Premier was half full; no children to be seen or heard, but many couples in their golden years fishing, boating, and just being together. Premier Lake is not a well-known provincial park, but in my opinion it contains some of the best scenery in B.C. and provides a tranquil camping experience adjacent to quiet, emerald green waters, ideal for the romantic.

History

The park was created in 1940 and was named in honour of William Smithe, premier of B.C. from 1883 to 1887, who visited the area in 1886. Long before this time the area was a camping location for the Ktunaxa people. BC Parks information leaflets state that "facilities in the park have been built above ground because of the archaeological significance of the area," but when I visited I could not see any evidence of this.

Location

The park is 72 kilometres north of Cranbrook, 45 kilometres northeast of Kimberley, in the Rocky Mountains. It encompasses 662 hectares, including six lakes of varying sizes—Premier, Canuck, Yankee, Cats Eye, Turtle, and Quartz—in a semi-remote wilderness. Access to the park is from Highway 93/95 1 kilometre north of Skookumchuk (a Chinook word you want to say over and over again, which means "strong and turbulent water"). The paved access road turns to gravel 5 kilometres before the campground but is still suitable for RVs and trailers if you're cautious. From this high section of the road you get your first glimpse of the lake's amazing colour and the fun that awaits. Services including a restaurant, gas station, and store are available at Skookumchuk.

Facilities

There are 57 sites in three adjacent campgrounds in a wooded area of western larch, cottonwood, and aspen. The sites are quite close together, but private. Some have tent pads while others are close to a babbling creek (a great on-site refrigeration system for cooling cans and bottles of drinks). Reservations are accepted, and all but the largest RV can be accommodated. Campsite 46 is wheelchair accessible with modified table and adjacent toilet. The park does not have flush toilets or a sani-station. A manually operated solar shower is provided near campsite 22. This consists of a black plastic bag you fill with water and leave in the sun for three hours. Then hang it in a wooden shower box (which resembles a pit toilet from the outside) and shower underneath it. An excellent economical idea. Why don't all BC Parks introduce these? Water is obtained from a pump and firewood is delivered to your site. There is also a volunteer park host, who in my opinion must have one of the best volunteer jobs in all of B.C.

Recreational Activities

Hiking

A number of easy trails have been constructed so campers can access the park's six lakes. A 20-minute trail

Solar shower, a unique experience.

leads to Cats Eye Lake, a 30-minute trail to Turtle Lake, a 45-minute trail to Yankee Lake, and a 45-minute trail to Quartz Lake (all distances one way). In addition, the Yankee/Canuck Loop Trail (two hours return) takes you to Turtle, Canuck, and Yankee Lakes. Those wanting day hikes have the option of hiking the Saddle Back Trail or making their way up to Premier Ridge or Quartz Lake. One of the easiest, shortest walks is the Staple Creek Trail from the centre of the campground to a trout spawning area (see below).

Fishing

The lakes have a good reputation amongst anglers for eastern brook trout and Gerrard.

Boating

There is a concrete boat launch in the day-use area at Premier Lake. Water-skiing is not permitted at the southern end of the lake (which is a bonus for those on the shoreline who want a quiet picnic), and boat speed is limited to 16 kilometres an hour.

Wildlife observation

There is a variety of wildlife here. To the west, Premier Ridge is an important winter habitat for elk, white-tailed deer, mule deer, and bighorn sheep. On the hillside west of Canuck Lake you can see salt licks that are often visited by these mammals. Cougars and bears also inhabit the region. Bird life includes eagles, herons, ospreys, kingfishers, loons, and numerous ducks and waterfowl.

One of the most inter-
esting sights in the park is
the fish hatchery. This is set
up with clear, concise interpretative boards that detail
the spawning process. I
learned that the Premier
Lake hatchery collects three
million eggs annually (do
you ever wonder whose job
it is to count them?), including 40 percent of the
rainbow trout eggs required
for the provincial egg hatchery system. Of those three
million eggs, 97 percent are
collected from wild fish, and
most of the offspring are
returned to the wild. After
the eggs hatch, the fish are
reared in the Kootenay Lake
Hatchery (also open to the
public), south of the park,
and then distributed to over
350 lakes and streams in the
province. It's amazing to

*Fish ladder at
Premier Lake Fish Hatchery.*

think a little trout that gets its start in life at Premier Lake and grows up
down the road may live out most of its existence in a lake north of Prince
George, hundreds of miles away, only to be caught and eaten by an angler
from another continent.

Family activities

I do not regard this as a family campground, although there is a small
gravel/sandy beach and the wooden wharves provide a good enclosed
swimming area. BC Parks warns of the dangers of swimmers itch here,
especially in July and August, so you should rinse off in clean water
immediately after swimming, and towel dry vigorously. There is an
adventure playground, a horseshoe pitch, and a grassy playing field.

Activities adjacent to the park

Two other provincial parks in the vicinity are well worth a visit, especially
if your passion is fishing. These are Whiteswan Lake (see Chapter 4), which
has camping facilities, and Top of the World (no developed camping). The
town of Kimberley to the south is a delightful community to wander

around, with a strong Bavarian influence. In addition, I cannot recommend Fort Steele Heritage Town (see Wasa Lake Provincial Park, Chapter 2) too highly.

Summary

When I stayed here I think my partner and I were the youngest by about twenty years (and we were definitely the only ones in a tent). My impression of Premier is that it is a campground for adults whose offspring have long gone and who are now rediscovering the joy of each other. The scenery is spectacular and tranquil. We spent our time swimming in the cold, clear waters of Premier Lake, much to the entertainment of the few other onlookers who were not brave enough (or were considerably wiser than we were) to experience the cool temperatures. Then we had lunch at the shaded picnic tables by the edge of the emerald waters, watching the fish jump. In the late afternoon we pitched tent and woke the next day with sun on the tent, surrounded by the heady smells of juniper and wild roses. Is it any wonder I consider Premier an idyllic paradise? It's one of the best campgrounds in B.C. if you yearn for a quiet camping experience with the one you love.

The tranquility at Premier Lake leaves a lasting impression.

27. Paarens Beach/Sowchea

I'm including two provincial parks under one heading so I can provide information on two little-known parks with a number of similar characteristics, located only 5 kilometres apart. I stayed at Sowchea a couple of years ago, preferring it to Paarens Beach only because all the campsites overlook the water. Some BC Parks literature classifies Sowchea as a Recreational Area, with fewer attributes than Paarens Beach Provincial Park, but I did not find this to be the case. BC Parks representatives readily acknowledge that although they are less than two hours from Prince George, few people seem aware of these two campgrounds. They are, however, scenic, tranquil environments for romantics in the know.

History

The campgrounds are close to the historic settlement of Fort St James, one of the first fur trading posts in B.C. Simon Fraser founded the fort in 1806 as the headquarters of New Caledonia. It became an important trading post for fur and manufactured goods, but was also subject to harsh winters that earned it the nickname "Siberia of the fur trade." The fort was operational throughout the nineteenth century, first run by the North West Company and then taken over by the Hudson's Bay Company, and into the early twentieth century. Today it operates as a national park (see below). Prior to Fraser's arrival the area was inhabited by the Carrier (Dakelh) people, so called because a widowed woman carried her husband's cremated remains in a small pouch until a potlatch ceremony could take place. Fraser, like a number of men stationed in this outpost, married or "entered upon the matrimonial state with" a Carrier woman.

Location

Paarens Beach Provincial Park is found west off Highway 27, 57 kilometres north of Vanderhoof and 15 kilometres west of Fort St James on Sowchea Road. Sowchea Provincial Park is located 5 kilometres farther along the same paved road. Both are at the south end of 100-kilometre Stuart Lake, amidst the Nechacko Plateau Hills. All services are available in Fort St James, a fifteen-minute drive from the parks.

Facilities

Paarens Beach has 36 camping spaces, of which six are close to the water, ideal for those with children. All are large and private, set in a lightly forested area. There is a sani-station and pit toilets. Sowchea has 30 sites, all close to the water of Stuart Lake amongst trees and thick ground vegetation. Like Paarens Beach, Sowchea only has basic facilities (pit toilets, water, firewood, picnic tables, fire pit). Only Paarens Beach accepts reservations, and neither campsite is wheelchair accessible.

Recreational Activities

Hiking

There are no hiking trails in either park, although you can take a nice stroll along the edge of Stuart Lake. Those who wish to tackle a serious hike should head towards Mount Pope, 5 kilometres northwest of Fort St James on Stones Bay Road. Here a route leads up to an old forestry lookout building with great views of Stuart Lake and the surrounding mountains (four to five hours return). Be warned: Mount Pope is the highest point in the area, 1472 metres up, so expect a good aerobic workout on this four- to five-hour return trip.

Fishing

Anglers go crazy here as the Stuart-Trembleur-Takla Lake chain offers over 180 kilometres of some of the finest rainbow trout fishing in B.C. Lake char, burbot, and kokanee can also be "easily" caught in Stuart Lake.

Boating

There are concrete boat launches at both campgrounds. The lake is an ideal location for canoeing, kayaking, sailing, and windsurfing, though you should bear in mind that it is subject to strong winds and sudden storms. Be cautious.

Family activities

Both parks have stretches of wide sandy beaches, and Paarens Beach has the added advantage of a change house and log picnic shelter. While the waters are somewhat cool, they are very close to the campground. At certain times of the year swimmers itch is a problem here; check the park notice board to see if it is prevalent when you arrive. Cycling between

Stuart Lake from Sowchea Provincial Park.

the two campgrounds or into Fort St James is an option for the entire family, as the roads are quiet and relatively flat.

Activities adjacent to the park

Both campgrounds are ideal bases from which to explore Fort St James National Historical Park. Similar to Barkerville or Fort Steele, this is a meticulously restored replica of Simon Fraser's fort, with some original buildings dating back to the 1880s—a general warehouse, fur store, and men's residence. Other outdoor displays show how the Carrier people smoked and dried salmon. Staff in period costume are available in each of the buildings to answer questions and provide details of these early pioneer times. The only limitation I could find at this informative interpretative museum was its lack of coffee bar/restaurant facilities. The town of Fort St James had little to offer, although the lovely scenery makes up for this. Those who enjoy golf should check out the quaint nine-hole golf course with great views of Stuart Lake.

Summary

I stayed at Sowchea in early September when there were few visitors. After using a hibachi to cook dinner on the beach, we walked along the water's edge, which was quite a tricky process as the sky grew darker because numerous boat ropes lay across our path. What I remember most about the campground was the sunsets and the stars. Despite receiving numerous warnings about the winds of Stuart Lake, our time there was tranquil and by 9:30 p.m. we could lie on our backs in the sand and watch the stars appear in their millions.

Additional Recommendations

The Best Hidden Gem Campgrounds See Chapter 5.
Whiteswan Lake See Chapter 4.
Conkle Lake (Okanagan). Accessed from a rough road unsuitable for low loaders, this remote lakeside spot has 34 camp spots and beautiful views of the lake.
Boya Lake (North by Northwest) This remote, aquamarine-coloured lake is the perfect place for romance. There are 44 sites available.
Exchamsiks River (North by Northwest). Camp amongst old-growth forest or on the beach of a fast-flowing river. Relax, unwind, and gaze in awe at the wonderful scenery around this twenty-site campground.
Kleanza Creek (North by Northwest) A tranquil campground close to a babbling, fish-spawning river where you can pan for gold. Twenty-one shaded camping spots are available.

THE BEST ADVENTURE CAMPGROUNDS

If you want more than just a place to pitch a tent within a provincial park, the campgrounds detailed in this section offer adventures in canoeing, fishing, diving, and mountain biking. While they were selected for their adventure offerings, each of these parks can be enjoyed by those who don't want to purchase a mountain bike, undertake a major canoe trip, or spend hundreds of dollars on diving or fishing equipment.

Bowron Lake Provincial Park is one of the most famous parks in the province, world renowned for its canoe circuit, and is primarily a campground for those who adore this sport. In contrast, Otter Lake is a perfect family campground, but its proximity to the Kettle Valley Mountain Bike Trail makes it an excellent venue for those who seek enjoyment in the saddle. Selecting the best fishing campground was almost impossible. I am not an angler, and BC Parks has numerous fishing hot spots, with all BC Parks employees claiming the best spot is in their jurisdiction. I finally chose Meziadin, not only for its reputed angling potential but also for the scenery and wildlife-viewing opportunities close by. Finally, Ellison is a wonderful campground for visitors of any age, with the additional draw of freshwater diving potential. If you are adventuring at Bowron Lake, Otter Lake, or Ellison you can rent the appropriate equipment nearby.

28. Bowron Lake

Any B.C. guidebook worth its salt must include reference to the 121,600-hectare wilderness of Bowron Lake Provincial Park, probably the provincial park most widely known outside B.C.'s borders. Its fame stems from a 116-kilometre canoe circuit described as "physically challenging but spiritually rewarding"—a magnet for all paddlers. The circuit has been featured in television documentaries screened all over the globe. This world-renowned adventure involves six large lakes (Bowron, Indianpoint, Isaac, Lanezi, Sandy, and Spectacle), a number of smaller lakes, the Bowron and Cariboo Rivers, and several small streams and portages. Paddlers can complete the route in six or seven days (racers can do it in one to two days) although many take ten days to complete it so they can fully appreciate the splendour of the Cariboo Mountains in which the roughly rectangular system of lakes is found. The Bowron Lake circuit provides a paddling adventure within a pristine wildlife sanctuary. The only drawback is its popularity, which has resulted in a restriction to the number of people allowed in the area. Anyone wishing to canoe the circuit (or the shorter western route) must register and pay the appropriate fee (see below). You can make advance reservations by calling (250) 992-3111. Those who are not canoeists should still make the effort to visit Bowron Lake as the camping, tranquillity, and scenery are first rate.

History

The park is situated between the ancestral lands of the Shuswap (Secwepemc) and Carrier (Dakelh) people. Evidence of ten pit houses has been found near where Bowron River flows into Bowron Lake, suggesting that in the past this may have been a year-round location for one of these First Nations communities. The park is named after John

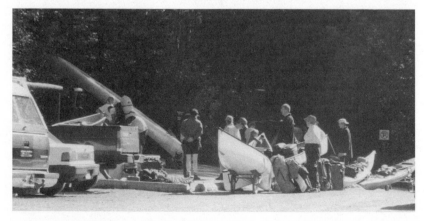

A group of canoeists at Bowron Lake getting ready to leave on the circuit.

Bowron (1837-1906), gold commissioner, government agent, and postmaster in the town of Barkerville (see Chapter 1). Gold deposits were never found at Bowron, so this area, although only 25 kilometres from the gold centre of Barkerville, remained untouched by prospectors. Around 1900 an American from Montana, Frank Kibbee moved here, becoming the first non-Native inhabitant of the area. A few more trappers and hunters moved into the area, and in the 1920s Thomas and Eleanor McCabe arrived from the U.S. The McCabes were quite wealthy and keen on wildlife. They passed their days studying the many birds and animals of the area. By 1925 they succeeded in persuading the B.C. government to establish a game reserve encompassing much of the land that is now a park, thereby planting the seeds for its ultimate destiny. In 1956, following the B.C. Power Commission decision not to use the lakes to generate power, discussions to establish a provincial park in the area began. In June 1961 it was awarded this status.

Location

The Bowron Lake Campground and main entrance to the park are found approximately 120 kilometres east of Quesnel, 30 kilometres past the end of Highway 26 on a good gravel road. The community of Wells is located almost 30 kilometres from the park and has all services, while Becker's Lodge and Bowron Lake Lodge near the park entrance have privately operated facilities including canoe and boat rentals, supplies, accommodation, and meals. (Becker's Lodge has a fantastic evening meal menu.)

Facilities

The primary campground is 1.5 kilometres from the park entrance and can accommodate 25 vehicles/tents. The facilities are basic (pit toilets, wood, water, fire pits, picnic tables) and reservations are accepted, but not through the Discover Camping reservation system. Instead, telephone (250) 992-3111. In addition to this main campground, there are wilderness camping locations throughout the canoe circuit with five to ten spaces, fire pits, pit toilets, and bear caches. There are also four rustic log shelters equipped with woodstoves for cooking and drying gear, and eight rustic cabins. Six radiophones for use in an emergency have also been placed on the circuit.

Recreational activities

Canoeing

Anyone planning to undertake the full 116.2-kilometre Bowron Lake circuit, or the smaller west-side route on Bowron Lake as far as Spectacle Lake (an easy day's journey with no portages), should collect information leaflets

*An excellent example of a "bear cache." Be sure to use one
when canoeing or even camping in bear country.*

on the excursion from the park office. Each leaflet contains a map showing campgrounds, distances, shelters, and portages. In addition to this summary information, there are also a number of specialist canoe/kayak texts written by paddling enthusiasts who describe the excursion in minuscule detail, while Richard Wright's book *Bowron Lake Provincial Park: The All-Seasons Guide* (published by Heritage House) gives comprehensive details of the entire park, including the canoe circuit. Novices can complete the circuit as long as they are fit and have adequate provisions and equipment. Upon registering at the park's visitors centre, all canoeists are shown a video of what to expect and are given a briefing by BC Parks staff. There are 9 kilometres of portages, and wheeled carriers can be used on all of them. The 16 kilometres of river paddling include rapids, which can be quite foreboding. These rapids, together with deadheads and thick reedbeds, are the primary hazards, although winds and inclement weather may also act as more persistent deterrents. The busiest time to travel is from late June until early August; one writer observes that the crowding can be annoying, but the compensation is the scenery and the camaraderie that occurs as paddlers from around the world congregate to experience this wilderness. According to the paddling community, the best time to complete the circuit is September, when the colours of the trees are spectacular and the crowds are gone. Be prepared for rain at any time of the year and for some cold nights.

You must make a reservation to canoe the circuit. In 1998 the group rate (7 to 14 people) for the full circuit was $180; canoe rate was $60 (2

or more people) or $50 (single occupant). Groups wishing to canoe just
the west side pay $118; everyone else, $38. Reservations can be made up
to a year in advance for any time between June and late October. A
maximum of 50 people is allowed to depart each day, with Saturday and
Sunday being the most popular times of departure.

Fishing

Rainbow trout are available in all lakes, though BC Parks says the best
fishing is at Bowron, Indianpoint, and Isaac Lakes. There are also Dolly
Varden, lake trout, Rocky Mountain whitefish, and kokanee (which are
running in Bowron Lake in late June/early July).

Wildlife viewing

As a wildlife sanctuary, Bowron Lake has an abundance to offer. Black
bears, moose, porcupines, beavers, and muskrats all inhabit the areas near
the lakes, while grizzly bears, caribou, and goats can be seen at the higher
elevations.

Family activities

The campground is primarily used by people embarking on or finishing
the canoe circuit, so there are few recreational pursuits for the family.
However, the safe, quiet, gravel roads are ideal for cycling, and canoeing
can be immensely enjoyable for young children (make sure you have
appropriate life jackets and safety equipment).

Activities adjacent to the park

The B.C.-government-administered community of Barkerville is a
reconstructed historical town that is delightful to explore and a real
contrast to ten days' paddling at Bowron Lake (see Chapter 1), while the
nearby town of Wells has a number of quaint historical buildings, many
recently restored. As the area is rich in gold-prospecting history you may
wish to try your luck at gold panning, an activity that requires a lot less
physical energy than canoeing and is a great way to unwind.

Summary

While researching this book I learned that the clearcut logging which
occurred around Bowron is one of only two human "constructions" visible
from space (the other is the Great Wall of China). This large clearcut,
which was carried out because of an insect infestation according to
foresters, is now reputed to be the largest tree plantation in the world. I
have not canoed the circuit but have camped in the park, enjoyed swimming
in the lake, and savoured dinner at the Becker's Lodge restaurant, so can
recommend this campground as one to be enjoyed by adventurers and
non-adventurers alike.

29. Otter Lake

This is one of the quieter campgrounds of the Okanagan but is still popular with those who know it and, since the development of the Kettle Valley Mountain Bike Trail, with those who love mountain biking. One of the reasons I love this campground is for the drive from the nearest large town, Princeton. Travellers follow a twisting mountain road through the Cascade Mountains, overlooking canyons and gorges, then on down to the edge of the tumbling Tulameen River. It's a breathtaking route, worth experiencing even if you do not intend to camp. Otter Lake is also within easy reach (a four- to five-hour drive) of the Lower Mainland, so it provides a quiet weekend getaway for people in Vancouver who know of its charms.

History

Otter Lake is an ideal base from which to explore the mining history of the Tulameen region. The town of Tulameen (which is a Native name meaning "red earth"), 5 kilometres south of the campground, was first used by Native people for hunting and fishing, then explored by gold miners in the 1800s. The Hudson's Bay Company used a road that passed through Tulameen, calling the settlement "encampment des femmes" as it was populated primarily by women waiting for their men to return from trapping and hunting. The town of Coalmont, just south of the park, is another gold-rush town. In 1925 it was the region's largest coal producer with an output of 100,000 tons. By 1940 the mine was exhausted and most residents moved away. Today Coalmont contains a café, general store,

Take time out to explore the Coalmont General Store, en route to Otter Lake.

and hotel—painted bright pink so you can't miss it—dating back to 1912. This formidable building is slowly being renovated, and when I visited the facilities and service it provided were somewhat disorganized. The park was established in 1963.

Location

The 51-hectare park is actually divided into two sections: a day-use area complete with beach and picnic tables in the community of Tulameen, and the camping section a ten-minute drive away along the banks of the lake. The campground is located 47 kilometres northwest of Princeton off Highway 5A, on a paved access road that runs toward the community of Coalmont. You can also reach it by turning off Highway 5A just south of the junction with Highway 97C south of Merritt. I have not taken this route so cannot comment on how friendly the 43 kilometres of gravel road are to cars or RVs. All services are available in Princeton, and there are a few general stores in Coalmont and Tulameen.

Facilities

Otter Lake is an ideal size, boasting 45 beautifully spaced, shady, large camping spots on the northwest shore of the lake, some with views of the water. All spaces can accommodate every size of RV or trailer. There are flush and pit toilets but no sani-station or showers. The park is wheelchair accessible and accepts reservations.

The Coalmont Hotel, painted bright pink, is in the process of being renovated.

Recreational Activities

Cycling

One of the most popular activities for every age here must be cycling. The route of the old Kettle Valley Railway, which operated from 1916 to 1962 and covered over 600 kilometres, now serves as the Kettle Valley Mountain Bike Trail. The trail runs through the valley near the provincial park and you can access it from many points along Highway 3. For those who arrive without wheels, bikes can be rented at a quaint outlet in Tulameen for $5 per hour or $20 per day for mountain bikes and tandems, $3.50 per hour or $14 per day for children's bikes (1998 rates). The Kettle Valley Trail leads into Princeton and is a flat, easy, scenic ride. Serious mountain bikers should read *Cycling the Kettle Valley Railway* by Dan and Sandra Langford (published by Rocky Mountain Books of Calgary) for an in-depth account of the route.

Hiking

A few trails wend their way through the park, but when I stayed, one of the most popular walks was along the gravel road leading to the community of Tulameen.

Fishing

The lake yields good fishing, especially for large rainbow trout, as indeed do other lakes in the area including Thynne, Allison (with provincial park camping facilities off Highway 5A), Osprey, and Tepee Lakes. All are in easy reach of Princeton.

Boating

There is a boat launch in the park, and all types of boats are permitted on the lake.

Wildlife viewing

Otters (surprise surprise!), beavers, red squirrels, mountain goats, cougars, and grizzly bears all inhabit the area. In 1997 a woman from Princeton was attacked and killed by a cougar while protecting her son. This catastrophe serves as a reminder for all to be vigilant while exploring B.C.'s wilderness.

Family activities

The 5 kilometres of Otter Lake permit easy access to water-based activities. It's possible to swim from a sandy beach (which in May and early June may not be visible if the lake waters are high). There are beaches both at the campground and in the day-use area, and there is a horseshoe pit at the campground.

Enjoy water activities at Otter Lake.

Activities adjacent to the park

You can while away the hours prospecting for gold in this region, and the pastime may also prove profitable. If you want to spend some time indoors, the town of Princeton, located where the Tulameen and Similkameen Rivers meet and named to honour the Prince of Wales' visit to Canada in 1860, has a pioneer museum and archive. In addition to artefacts from local First Nations and early European settlers, it contains items from the Chinese people who played an integral part in the early development of mining and railway construction in the region. If you're looking for a picturesque place to eat on your way to or from the park, consider the Bromley Station Pub, perched high on the mountainside just outside Princeton on the Hope road. It has a family room, good food, and eye-catching views from the outdoor patio to the valley below.

Summary

A word of warning: If you have not cycled for awhile, consider renting bikes for just a few hours and not an entire day. I believe I am quite fit, but my poor bottom was sore for days when I decided to get my dollar's worth and spent eight hours in the saddle. In retrospect, the experience and scenery (and pain) were well worth it, as the recently developed Kettle Valley Trail is a super route. There are plans to make it part of the Trans-Canada Trail, which will cross Canada by the year 2000.

30. Meziadin Lake

If you are heading north on Highway 37, the Stewart-Cassiar Highway, Meziadin Lake is the first provincial park you reach. Set amongst the beautiful Coast Mountains by the side of a lake, this provincial park is used by two types of campers: those who adore fishing who settle here for days (but wish it were a lifetime), and those who are travelling up (or down) the partly paved Cassiar Highway. I fell into the second category when I stayed here one September night on my journey north to Whitehorse. It rained torrents, but despite this experience I regard it as one of the better "off the beaten track" campgrounds because of its beautiful location and the wildlife-viewing opportunities close at hand. Anglers have an additional reason to love this remote wilderness: its excellent fishing.

History

The area south of the campground is rich in First Nations history. The Kitwanga Fort National Heritage Site and the communities of Gitwangak, Gitanyow (formerly Kitwancool), Gitsegukla, and Kispiox, north of the junction of Highway 37 and Highway 16, all have totem poles, old buildings, and historical markers detailing the history of the Gitksan people of the area. Gitanyow (meaning "awesome warrior people") has a collection of eighteen totem poles, some over 100 years old. It is well worth taking the time to detour to these impressive monuments. The Stewart-Cassiar Highway was built in sections over many years and finally completed in 1972. Today it is becoming a popular tourist route (expect to see more RVs than trucks or cars in the summer) and is gradually being paved.

Meziadin Lake.

Location

Meziadin Lake Provincial Park is located about two hours north (156 kilometres) of Kitwanga junction (Highways 37 and 16) on Highway 37, a couple of kilometres south of Meziadin Junction, where you will find a small coffee bar/restaurant (do not expect great culinary delights), a shop, and gas.

Facilities

The park has 46 open gravel campsites affording little privacy, though they have good views, are well spaced, and can accommodate all sizes of vehicles. A few sites are situated on the lakeshore. There is no sani-station, and garbage has to be stored in the only concrete structure on the site because of the prevalence of bears in the area. All eating, cooking, and drinking utensils must be kept in a vehicle day and night. There is limited access for disabled people, and facilities are the basic ones found in B.C. parks (firewood, picnic tables, fire pit, water, and pit toilets).

Recreational Activities

Fishing

As mentioned above, this is an angler's dream location for both bait- and fly-fishing enthusiasts. When I stayed, the campground was empty from 6:00 a.m. until 9:00 p.m. as all occupants seemed to be out fishing. There are lots of rainbow trout to catch, although the sizes are not great (14 to 16 inches), while whitefish and larger Dolly Varden are also common catches in Meziadin Lake. I was told by Sam, who offered us shelter from the pouring rain in his RV during our last stay, that the best fishing is from the gravel bars at the mouths of the creeks that enter the lake, with Henna and Tintina Creek being particularly rewarding. Although it is possible to fish in waders from the campground, a boat allows you to explore the creeks flowing into the lake, where fish seem to congregate. Bears also recognize these as productive fishing areas, so take care!

Hiking

There are no developed trails leading from the campground. Those who seek serious excursions on foot should head north on Highway 37 to Mount Edziza Provincial Park. You need to be experienced for this backcountry wilderness. For campers seeking a good day-hike, a trail from Strohn Lake, west of Meziadin Lake on the Stewart Road, leads to Bear Glacier (24 kilometres return).

Boating

A modern boat launch is located in the park, and all types of boats are permitted on the lake. It is wonderfully relaxing to canoe here.

The trail from Strohn Lake leads to the Bear Glacier.

Wildlife viewing

My most vivid memory of Meziadin Lake is of the live bear trap kept at the park. BC Parks officials told me it had not been used recently...but black and grizzly bears *are* common in the area, as are mountain sheep, caribou, wolves, moose, and beaver. At the southern end of Meziadin Lake, where the Nass River flows in, a fish ladder has been constructed, and more than a quarter of a million salmon travel through here between July and September. Watch for huge fish leaping up the ladder if you visit during these months.

Family activities

There are few family activities here, so unless your offspring are avid fishers or wildlife watchers, my advice would be for you to take the kids to another campsite for any stay longer than an overnight stop.

Activities adjacent to the park

Anyone camping at Meziadin *must* make the 67-kilometre journey from Meziadin Junction to Stewart, Canada's most northerly ice-free port at the end of the Portland Canal. I believe this road is one of the most breathtaking in the province; every time you round a corner it seems another glacier is revealed, over 20 in total including the Bear Glacier. The road passes within a few feet of this glacier, then proceeds through a granite canyon by the waters of Bear River and on to Stewart, The community of Stewart has some trendy little coffee bars, tourist information, and pretty buildings. In the early 1900s, 10,000 people lived in the area to mine gold and silver, but now the population is only 1000 (including zealous RCMP officers who monitor road speeds carefully—be warned). The films *Bear Island*, *The Thing*, and *Iceman* have recently been filmed at this location.

Three kilometres farther along the road is Hyder, USA, which has little to offer other than a couple of bars. If you're visiting in August/September, however, take the gravel road out of Hyder for approximately 5 kilometres till you reach Fish Creek, where you will have a good chance of seeing black and grizzly bears feeding on the salmon that fill the waters. United States Park officials patrol this area and provide information for tourists. They have even named some of the bears that frequent the area. In the specially constructed viewing areas you are only a few feet away from the bears, who are splashing through the water after salmon. The sound of ripping flesh is easily audible as these magnificent creatures devour their catch. During our three-hour visit in September we saw fifteen different black and grizzly bears, including a mother and two cubs. Bald eagles also inhabit the region. This is an unforgettable excursion.

Summary

Meziadin is one of only three provincial parks on the Cassiar Highway. All appear strategically placed to accommodate the travelling camper. Kinaskan Lake Provincial Park is about three hours' drive from Meziadin. It was the perfect lunch spot for us as we drove north, but it does boast 50 campsites on the shore of a lake with reputedly excellent fishing (including two-pound rainbow trout). It's an ideal place to rest, especially as by this time Highway 37 has become a gravel road, so aching, well-bounced muscles need to be stretched. The third campground is at sensational Boya Lake, 34 kilometres south of the Cassiar-Alaska Highway junction and a full day's drive from Meziadin Lake. With 44 spaces by the side of a milky-blue glacial lake and stunning views of the Cassiar Mountains, this is a wonderful place to camp and reflect on the day's journey. While I did not find Meziadin Lake busy (perhaps because of the rain), BC Parks warns that it can be, so arrive early or be prepared for disappointment. Also be aware that summer temperatures are never high, so dress accordingly, but do make the effort to visit.

31. Ellison

Famous for having Canada's only freshwater dive park, Ellison must also rank as one of the best campgrounds in the Okanagan, primarily because it does not feel as busy as many of the others in the region and therefore offers a quieter family camping experience. Although only 16 kilometres away from a major centre of population, it does not suffer from the constant hum of traffic as other popular parks in the Okanagan do (e.g., Haynes Point, Okanagan Lake). It is nestled into a forest on the northeastern shore of Okanagan Lake in one of the warmest areas of the province, which makes it easy to see why campers return here for a week or more at a time. Every age group can enjoy this idyllic spot from April to October.

History

This area owes its development to a man named Cornelius O'Keefe, who in the nineteenth century was driving cattle from Oregon to the hungry men in the gold-mining areas of the Cariboo when he discovered a fertile grassland at the north end of Okanagan Lake. He decided not to drive cattle but to raise them in this location, and built a ranch, still in existence today (see below). In 1962, over a hundred years after O'Keefe first travelled the area, Ellison Provincial Park was created.

Location

The provincial park is located 16 kilometres south of Vernon on the northeast shore of Okanagan Lake. Signposts in Vernon indicate which road to take to get to Ellison. After leaving the town the lakeside road

The beach at Ellison Provincial Park.

twists and turns past orchards, farms, and ranches that have been an integral part of the community for over a century. The park is situated in 200 hectares of forested beachland high above a shoreline of rocks, cliffs, beaches, scenic headlands, and tranquil coves. To the west are the rolling hills of the Thompson Plateau; to the east the Monashee Mountains. Ponderosa pine and Douglas fir are the dominant vegetation in the park.

Facilities

The 54 gravel camping spots located here are perfect. Some have views of the lake, a few have views of the adventure play area, and all are spacious and private to accommodate even the largest RV. There are flush and pit toilets, water, and wood but no sani-station or showers. The park is wheelchair accessible and reservations are accepted.

Recreational Activities

Diving

Otter Bay at Ellison is the home of Canada's only freshwater dive park. A number of objects and artefacts have been sunk here to attract fish and rubber-clad individuals. BC Parks says the area has "been enhanced to provide a variety of fish for snorkelling and scuba diving" but seems reluctant to specify how this enhancement has occurred. A change house with freshwater showers (cold) is located a short distance away from the sandy bay. For those of us who do not wish to try the activity, this is a great place to "diver watch," especially at the end of the day as night diving is popular. Campers wishing to rent diving equipment should contact Innerspace Dive and Kayak at 3306 32nd Avenue in Vernon, phone (250) 549-2040.

Hiking

Six kilometres of hiking trails wind their way through the park. Paved trails, a little steep in places, lead from the campground to the lakeside, while the popular Ellison Trail provides a 40-minute walk where explorers may see Columbian ground squirrels and even porcupines according to BC Parks literature. In addition, the Captains Cove Interpretative Trail gives details of First Nations and European history. BC Parks warns of rattlesnakes in the area (see below).

Fishing

For those without a boat, it is possible to catch carp, burbot, kokanee, Rocky Mountain whitefish, and large rainbow trout from the shoreline. However those with access to the waters are the true angling winners. Vernon's tourist board states there are over 100 lakes in which to fish, all less than one hour's drive from the city.

The amphitheatre at Ellison Provincial Park.

Boating

There is no boat launch in the park itself, but there is a public boat launch (signposted from the road) 6 kilometres north of the campground. Water-skiing, powerboating, and the ever-pestering jet-skiers are allowed on the lake, and mooring buoys are provided in South Bay and Otter Bay.

Family activities

The three protected beach areas with soft, peach-coloured sand are ideal places for swimming, sandcastle construction, and sunbathing. A change house is situated between the two coves (Otter Bay and South Cove), while a third swimming location is at Sandy Beach (this is the only beach that permits animals). The existence of three locations ensures you never feel crowded. When I visited, a volleyball net had been erected by Otter Bay. After a busy day swimming and sunbathing, children can find further entertainment in the adventure playground or playing ball games on the manicured playing field. This field has an underground sprinkler system and it looks like it should belong to an expensive Okanagan golf course rather than a B.C. provincial park. Interpretative programs are offered in the park amphitheatre from mid-June until Labour Day. One of the most popular is an evening of stargazing, as the clear Okanagan skies offer fantastic astronomical opportunities. The paved roads of the park are good cycling and rollerblading terrain.

Activities adjacent to the park

The community of Vernon, the oldest town in the province's Interior, dating back to 1892, is only 16 kilometres away and offers many "urban" pursuits.

These include a museum and archive, art gallery, golf and mini-golf, waterslides, and leisure centres. At historic O'Keefe Ranch, 12 kilometres north of Vernon, there are tours of the O'Keefe mansion, preserved and restored heritage buildings (including a picture-postcard church), a huge model railway display, tons of cowboy memorabilia, a picnic area, restaurant, and gift shop. There are also a number of farm animals to add further authenticity to this 1867 abode. For the thirsty, the Okanagan Springs Brewery in Vernon offers tours during the summer months.

Summary

I last visited this park in early May, arriving around 5:00 p.m. as storm clouds drifted over and claps of thunder from across the lake threatened our plans. After a few large raindrops fell, the clouds moved on and the perfect camping experience awaited. Despite its proximity to Vernon, one of this campground's biggest advantages is its "away from it all" feel. BC Parks warns of hazards such as swimmers itch, poison ivy, steep cliffs, and rattlesnakes. The information on the reptiles reveals they rarely bite except when they are handled or stepped on, so your best bet is to resist that burning desire you may have to step on one. If by chance you or your loved one is unfortunate enough to be bitten, do not apply a tourniquet or cut the wound or try to suck the poison out (that is to say, do not follow the methods advocated in most cowboy films), but rather go to the nearest hospital. While rattlesnake bites are painful, they are rarely fatal, so rest assured you'll live to tell the tale.

Additional Recommendations

The Best Hiking Campgrounds See Chapter 3.

Champion Lakes (Kootenay Country) This park has excellent canoeing potential, 95 camping spots, and an idyllic setting high in the Selkirk Mountains.

Cathedral (Okanagan) This is a relatively small, 16-space campground with only wilderness camping available but with access to some fantastic hikes in the backcountry.

THE BEST FORESTRY CAMPGROUNDS

The BC Forestry Service (BCFS) administers over 1400 campgrounds that provide approximately 12,000 rustic campsites for wilderness camping adventures in what are often remote, beautifully scenic areas far from main roads and centres of population. Until 1998 the BCFS facilities were free, but in 1999 the Forestry Service introduced user fees for campers using the sites. The BCFS sells an annual pass for $27 ($22 for seniors, including GST), which allows unlimited access to most BCFS sites. For those who do not wish to purchase the pass, a nightly fee of $8 will be charged for most sites.

There are about 30 heavily used campgrounds near urban areas that require security and additional maintenance (none of these campgrounds are included in this chapter). At these high-maintenance campgrounds the nightly fee is $10, and passholders will have to pay $5.

Passes are available from some sporting goods stores, from maintenance contractors at the BCFS sites, and from government agencies. For more information about the fees and for lists of campgrounds, see the BCFS website (http://www.for.gov.bc.ca).

What to expect at a BCFS campground

Anyone accustomed to camping in private or provincial park campgrounds, where fresh water, firewood, and regularly cleaned toilets (with copious quantities of toilet paper) are all taken for granted, should be prepared for a new experience when camping in a BCFS site. One of the biggest differences is the location and access of the sites. Most BCFS sites have

*Expect the facilities at Forestry campgrounds
to be more rustic and rudimentary.*

few or no formal road signposts indicating their existence, but you can find them by using the *British Columbia Recreational Atlas* or the free maps produced by the Ministry of Forests (available from the appropriate forestry regional office that administers the site(s) you are interested in—see the appendix), or by following instructions in books like this one. A good source of information is Cathy and Craig Copeland's *Camp Free in B.C.* (from Vancouver's Voice in the Wilderness Press), which describes over 250 forestry (previously free) campgrounds between the Trans-Canada Highway and the United States border, including campgrounds of the Rocky Mountains and Vancouver Island.

A large number of the BCFS campsites are on remote, twisting, potholed logging roads unsuitable for large RVs, trailers, or cars and therefore only accessible with a good four-wheel-drive or truck. Serious consideration has to be given to the wear and tear on the camper's vehicle, not to mention on the camping party.

The facilities offered at these sites are considerably more rudimentary than those in provincial parks, though the facilities and services offered vary between sites. The emphasis is on enjoyment and the experience of an isolated wilderness, not on developed facilities. The campgrounds tend to be small; it is quite unusual to find a BCFS site accommodating more than twenty vehicles, and most accommodate fewer than seven. It often appears that little planning has gone into arranging the camping spots themselves, and they may appear primitive and even scruffy to campers accustomed to provincial parks. On the other hand, some BCFS sites house more than twenty visitors and are almost of provincial park quality. There is usually at least one toilet (with or without toilet tissue, and with a door that might hang a foot above the ground) and wooden or concrete picnic tables, but not necessarily one per site. Water is frequently only available from adjacent rivers and streams. Some campsites have fire pits or a fire ring, firewood, and garbage cans; most do not. With a few exceptions they are not maintained, so they often unfortunately feature burnt garbage in the fire pit or elsewhere, left by unscrupulous users who have not followed the "pack out what you pack in" rule.

Most BCFS sites are located near a river, stream, or lake and draw the fishing enthusiasts who seek little in the way of organized activity or facilities other than the potential of a good catch. And

Expect to see this sign at BCFS sites.

all the campgrounds grant outdoor enthusiasts the chance to sleep amongst some of the most breathtaking scenery in the world.

What to take to a BCFS campground

What you pack for BCFS camping is much the same as what you need for provincial park camping, with a few additional supplies.

1. Drinking water. Often the only running water available is from creeks and streams, so ensure you have copious quantities of fresh water or can boil river water for at least five minutes before using it.
2. Garbage bags. BCFS does not provide staff to collect garbage and clean up sites, therefore it is up to you to pack out what you pack in.
3. Toilet paper.
4. Insect repellent.
5. Matches.
6. Firewood. If you intend to cook over a campfire, dry firewood is a must. Be sure to check that there is no campfire ban in the region you are visiting, and always ensure your fire is properly extinguished when you leave.
7. Picnic chairs. Often picnic tables are either not available or not plentiful, so carrying your own seats provides a more enjoyable camping experience.

Recommended forestry campsites

I've selected a few of the more easily accessible campgrounds in four areas of the province known for their outstanding natural beauty. I have to admit that unlike the other recommendations in this book, many of the suggestions in this chapter are not based on my own personal visits but have been taken from other guidebooks, the advice of friends, and information from representatives at BCFS regional offices.

Central B.C.

The **Nahatlatch River Recreational Site**, with a series of ten BCFS campgrounds, stretches along this beautiful river system between Harrison Lake and the Fraser Canyon on the east side of the Coast Mountains, an easy five-hour drive from the Lower Mainland. The fast-flowing white water of the Nahatlatch River runs through Nahatlatch, Hannah, and Frances Lakes and invites kayaking, rafting, and fishing. Generally the waters are too fast for swimming, although if you look hard there are some quieter backwater pools. The camping sites are situated along the Nahatlatch Forest Road. To reach them, turn west off the Trans-Canada Highway at the community of Boston Bar and drive through the town to cross the Fraser River Bridge. Head north on the West Side Road for 18 kilometres to the Nahatlatch River Bridge. Nahatlatch Forest Road runs for 20 kilometres west of the Nahatlatch River Bridge. The campgrounds are found along this road. Most spots are suitable for only one or two vehicles, although the final one, Squakium Creek, has ten spaces, all with fire pits. This final site is on a calm lake as opposed to being by the rushing waters. As you travel this road, watch for white-water rafters who frequent the river. On a note of caution, this area is prone to some very high summer temperatures, often between 30 and 40 degrees C, so remember to take the necessary precautions.

Kootenays

As I have said on numerous occasions, the Kootenays is my favourite region in B.C., primarily because it is so quiet, even in July and August. The three recommendations outlined below have been taken from *Camp Free in B.C.* and have also been mentioned by other travel writers.

Wilson Lake West Recreational Site, at the end of a narrow, steep-sided lake, is reached via an access road that is unsuitable for motorhomes and trailers. Go south from the town of Nakusp. At the junction where Highway 6 East and Highway 6 West meet, follow Highway 6 East for 7 kilometres, then turn left on Wilson Lake Road. After 5.3 kilometres turn right at the junction and proceed for another 2 kilometres, whereupon a sign directs you to Wilson Lake. There are two small campgrounds on the lake. Nakusp Beach on Upper Arrow Lake, a short drive from this secluded spot, has excellent swimming and sunbathing and great views.

Box Lake Recreational Site is larger and more easily accessible than Wilson Lake. From the Highway 6 East and West junction, travel south towards New Denver. After 7 kilometres, just past Wilson Lake Road, Box Lake will come into view. Look for a road on the right at the end of the lake. The quaint campground is a brief drive along this route.

Wragge Beach BCFS Site is situated on peaceful Slocan Lake, where you can sunbathe, swim, and fish. This is a popular campground for those "in the know." From the junction of Highways 6 and 31A in New Denver, head north 15 kilometres and turn left onto Bonanza Road. After 1 kilometre, turn on Shannon Creek Forest Service Road and proceed along this route, watching for signs on the left for Wragge Beach Road. After you see the sign, turn onto the road and continue on for 5 kilometres until you cross a creek, then travel a further 11 kilometres to Wragge Beach. Facilities here include picnic tables on the lakeshore, a day-use area, and beautiful beachside camping.

Northern B.C.

BCFS campgrounds are frequently used by anglers who have little interest in hiking, swimming, or other activities, preferring to sojourn near the fishing hot spots. Many of the forestry campgrounds in northern B.C., particularly around Prince George, are geared to the fishing community. Most are quite small, although some can accommodate ten or more camping parties.

One of the larger spots is **Summit Lake Recreational Site**, 2 kilometres west of Highway 97 on Caine Creek Road, 30 kilometres north of Prince George. It has space for almost 30 vehicles. While Summit Lake is the most easily accessible, other sites near Crooked River include **Crystal Lake**, **Emerald Lake**, **100 Road Bridge**, **Domino Lake**, **Merton Lake**, and **Davie Lake**. Approximately 90 kilometres north of Prince George is a circuit of lakes, all with their own campgrounds. **Goose Lake**, **Cat Lake**, **Hambone Lake**, and **Fishhook Lake** all have rudimentary camping, while larger **Tacheeda Lake** has a total of 28 vehicle/tent sites. For more detailed information contact the Prince George regional office of the Ministry of Forests at (250) 565-6193.

The Rockies

The Rockies are a magnet for campers, and for those who wish to travel off the beaten track, BCFS sites provide numerous wilderness camping adventures. All the recommendations below are suitable for all but the largest RV.

Wapiti Lake is a five-vehicle campground situated in a large grassy meadow overlooking the eastern shore of the lake. It is found off Highway

3/93 between Cranbrook and Fernie and offers a tranquil holiday escape. From the bridge over Kootenay River, southeast of Wadner, proceed uphill for 6 kilometres to a turnoff on the right of a dirt road. After less than 1 kilometre go right at the intersection, then right again at the T-junction. Another kilometre takes you to the lake, and the campground is located a further 1.5 kilometres along.

The Kootenay River Valley between the Purcell Mountains to the west and the Rocky Mountains to the east is a wonderful place for a camping vacation, and **Thunder Hill Park**, formerly a provincial park, is a convenient location from which to appreciate the mountains. The campground is easy to reach. Six kilometres northeast of Canal Flats, turn off Highway 93 to the west at a sign reading Blue Lake Forest Centre. The entrance to the ten-space site is immediately after the turn; consequently, the only disadvantage here may be the slight noise of traffic. Those who want to travel a little farther may decide to continue on to Findlay Creek Forest Services Road, another 8 kilometres along, to the small but quiet **Findlay Creek Recreational Site.**

Horseshoe Lake Recreational Site has a lot to offer, is easily accessible, and can accommodate at least ten camping parties. Situated on a lake beside the steeply rising Rocky Mountains, you can swim, mountain bike, hike, and fish here. From the historic town of Fort Steele, turn southeast off Highway 93/95 onto the Wadner-Fort Steele Road, on the east side of Kootenay River. Follow the river for 11 kilometres until a signpost on the left indicates you have reached Horseshoe Lake.

Typical signpost at a BCFS site.

APPENDIX: USEFUL ADDRESSES

The following pages contain suggestions for further information that will increase your appreciation of B.C. There are addresses of tourism associations, BC Parks and national parks administrative offices, BCFS regional offices, and other useful phone numbers or web sites to help you plan a successful camping adventure.

Tourism Associations

If you are considering a vacation in this part of the country, you should contact the regional tourism associations and ask for information on the areas you plan to visit and the recreational pursuits that are of specific interest. Information is provided free of charge from:

Tourism BC
PO Box 9830, Stn. Provincial Government
Victoria, BC V8W 9W5
Telephone: 1-800-663-6000

Thompson/Okanagan Tourism Association
1332 Water Street, Kelowna, BC V1Y 9P4
Telephone: 1-800-567-2275   Fax: (250) 861-7493

Cariboo Tourism Association
190 Yorston Street, PO Box 4900, Williams Lake, BC V2G 2V8
Telephone: 1-800-663-5885   Fax: (250) 392-2838

Northern B.C. Tourism Association
PO Box 1030, 11, 3167 Tatlow Road, Smithers, BC V0J 2N0
Telephone: 1-800-663-8843   Fax: (250) 847-4321

Peace River/Alaska Highway Tourism Association
9923-96 Avenue, Fort St John, BC V1J 4J3
Telephone: 1-888-785-2544   Fax: (250) 785-4424
E-mail: prahta@awinc.com

Tourism Rockies
PO Box 10, 1905 Warren Avenue, Kimberley, BC V1A 2Y5
Telephone: (250) 427-4838   Fax: (250) 427-3344
E-mail: bcrockies@cyberlink.bc.ca

BC Parks Offices

BC Parks produces leaflets on most of the larger provincial parks with campgrounds. These usually contain a map of the campsite and tell you where wood, toilets, water, etc., can be found. For many parks, details of the hiking trails (or in the case of Bowron Lake, the canoe circuit) are also given. Because these leaflets are available, I have not included maps in this book. I strongly urge you to write and request information on the park or parks you plan to visit.

In addition to the leaflets, BC Parks produces a number of other publications to add to your enjoyment of B.C. parks. These include: "Mountain Flowers of BC Provincial Parks," "Principal Trees of Provincial Parks," "Campground Critters of Provincial Parks," "Bears in Provincial Parks," "Principal Berries of Provincial Parks," and "Things to do Outdoors in BC Provincial Parks" (including a fascinating section on getting to know your ants). These information leaflets, together with information on specific campgrounds, can be collected from the visitors centres of larger parks or by writing directly to the regional director of the area of interest to you.

BC Parks Headquarters
The Information Officer, BC Parks
Second Floor, 800 Johnson Street, Victoria, BC V8V 1X4
Telephone: (250) 387-5002   Fax: (250) 387-5757

Thompson River District
Regional Director, BC Parks, 1210 McGill Road, Kamloops, BC V2C 6N6
Telephone: (250) 851-3000   Fax: (250) 828-4633

Okanagan District
Regional Director, BC Parks, Okanagan Lake Park, Box 399,
Summerland, BC V0H 1Z0
Telephone: (250) 494-6500   Fax: (250) 494-9737

West Kootenay District
Regional Director, BC Parks, Site 8, Comp 5, R.R. 3, Nelson, BC V1L 5P6
Telephone: (250) 825-3500   Fax: (250) 825-9509

East Kootenay District
Regional Director, BC Parks, Wasa Lake Park, Box 118, Wasa, BC V0B 2K0
Telephone: (250) 422-4200   Fax: (250) 422-3326

Skeena District
Regional Director, BC Parks, Bag 5000, 3790 Alfred Avenue,
Smithers, BC V0J 2N0
Telephone: (250) 847-7320   Fax: (250) 847-7659

Cariboo District
Regional Director, BC Parks, 181 First Avenue North
Williams Lake, BC V2G 1Y8
Telephone: (250) 398-4414   Fax: (250) 398-4686

Prince George District
Regional Director, BC Parks, Box 2045, 4051-18 Avenue
Prince George, BC V2N 2J6
Telephone: (250) 565-6340
Fax: (250) 565-6940

Peace-Liard District
Regional Director, BC Parks, 250, 10003-110 Avenue
Fort St John, BC V1J 6M7
Telephone: (250) 787-3407   Fax: (250) 787-3490

BC Parks information is also available on the internet at:
http://www.env.gov.bc.ca.

BC Ferries

Information and schedules for BC Ferries are available in Vancouver by
calling (604) 277-0277, in Victoria at (250) 381-5335, and elsewhere by
dialling 1-888-223-3779, by writing to BC Ferries at 1112 Fort Street,
Victoria, BC, V8V 4V2, or by visiting their web site at:
http://www.bcferries.bc.ca.

BCFS Campgrounds

The more than 1400 BCFS campgrounds are administered by 42 provincial
forest districts that are overseen by regional offices. Anyone planning to
visit these facilities is advised to contact the regional office for the area of
interest to obtain the relevant maps, or visit the BCFS web site at:
http://www.for.gov.bc.ca.

Cariboo Region
Ministry of Forests, 200, 640 Borland Street, Williams Lake, BC V2G 4T1
Telephone: (250) 398-4345
Information on the Chilcotin, Horsefly, 100 Mile House, Quesnel, and
Williams Lake.

Nelson Region
Ministry of Forests, 518 Lake Street, Nelson, BC V1L 4C6
Telephone: (250) 354-6200
Information on the Arrow Lakes, Boundary, Cranbrook, Golden, Invermere,
Kootenay, and Revelstoke.

Kamloops Region
Ministry of Forests, 515 Columbia Street, Kamloops, BC V2C 2T7
Telephone: (250) 828-4131
Information on Lillooet, Merritt, Princeton, Salmon Arm, and Vernon.

Prince George Region
Ministry of Forests, 1011-4 Avenue, Prince George, BC V2L 3H9
Telephone: (250) 565-6193
Information on Burns Lake, Houston, Fort St James, Vanderhoof, Mackenzie,
Fort Nelson, and Dawson Creek.

Prince Rupert Region
Ministry of Forests, Bag 5000, 3726 Albert Avenue, Smithers, BC V0J 2N0
Telephone: (250) 847-7500
Information on Cassiar, North Coast, Lower Stikine, Lakes District, Kispiox,
and Kalum.

National Parks
National Parks telephone number is 1-800-213-7275. The internet address
is: http://parkscanada.pch.gc.ca.

Yoho National Park
Box 99, Field, BC V0A 1G0
Telephone: (250) 343-6324

Kootenay National Park
Box 220, Radium Hot Springs, BC V0A 1M0
Telephone: (250) 347-9615

Glacier National Park (and Mount Robson Provincial Park)
Box 350, Revelstoke, BC V0E 2S0
Telephone: (250) 837-5255

Jayne Seagrave, the happy camper.

Jayne Seagrave lives in East Vancouver with her husband, Andrew Dewberry, and son Jack. She holds a Ph.D. in Criminology and divides her time between working as the marketing manager for The Vancouver Tool Corp, and camping, travelling, and exploring the province of British Columbia.

Look for Jayne's previous two books at your favourite bookstore. For a complete list of books available from Heritage House please visit our web site at www.heritagehouse.ca.